Bluffer's

GUIDE TO

BOND

MARK MASON

© Haynes Publishing 2020
First published March 2020

A CIP Catalogue record for this book
is available from the British Library.

ISBN: 978 1 78521 719 7

Library of Congress control no. 2019950386

Published by Haynes Publishing,
Sparkford, Yeovil, Somerset BA22 7JJ, UK.
Tel: 01963 440635
Int. tel: +44 1963 440635
Website: www.haynes.com

Printed in Malaysia.

Series Editor: David Allsop.

CONTENTS

As Bond's creator, Ian Fleming, said: 'The target of my books lay somewhere between the solar plexus and the upper thigh.'

THE NAME'S BOND . . .

Bond, as they say with each new film, is back. Nonsense. Bond never went away.

And what's more he never will, because James Bond is more than just a man, more even than a secret agent. James Bond is an eternal truth. To quote *The Sunday Times* book review of *On Her Majesty's Secret Service*, 'Bond is what every man would like to be, and what every woman would like between her sheets.' As Bond's creator, Ian Fleming, said: 'The target of my books lay somewhere between the solar plexus and the upper thigh.'

Bond is always in the collective consciousness, whether or not he's gracing the screen (silver or small), and whether or not we know what he'll look like next time. Each time a man approaches a bar to order a pint of beer, a tiny fragment of him fights the urge to make it a vodka martini. Each time a woman sitting at that bar senses the man turning to her, she dreams he will open with: 'The name's Bond, James Bond.'

Bond's life is the dream, the aspiration, the impossible goal. The tedious realities of everyday life make us yearn for a world like his, with exotic destinations, gambling, gold and girls; beaches instead of bosses, cocktails instead of cornflakes, spying instead of school-runs, adventure instead of alimony. And, when stuck behind a car that won't get out of the motorway's middle lane, who hasn't longed for a button on the dashboard that can fire a rocket up its exhaust?

But where others see an impossible goal as unachievable, the bluffer sees an opportunity. Educate yourself in 007 and you will always be guaranteed an audience. Others will know his name; you can tell them how he got that name. They will know that his martini is shaken, not stirred; you can tell them why. Arm yourself with the right facts, opinions and insider knowledge and you will become as irresistible as Bond himself. For when it comes to holding people's rapt attention, a Bond snippet is almost as effective as the business end of a Walther PPK.

This book sets out to guide you through the main danger zones encountered in discussions about Bond, and to equip you with a vocabulary and an evasive technique that will minimise the risk of being rumbled as a bluffer. It will lend you a few easy-to-learn hints and methods that will allow you to be accepted as a Bond aficionado of rare ability and experience. But it will do more. It will give you the tools to impress legions of marvelling listeners with your knowledge and insight about the world's most infamous spy – without anyone discovering that before reading it you didn't know the difference between a Pinaud Elixir and a Béarnaise sauce.

THE MAN

The weird thing about conversations concerning James Bond is that people talk about everything *except* James Bond. They rabbit on about his cars, his gadgets, his girls, his cocktails – everything, it seems, apart from the man himself. This is not to say that all the stuff surrounding him isn't interesting; of course it is. But if you really want to stand out in the Bond business, your secret weapon has to be the little-tackled question of 007's identity. Master this and you will deservedly be acknowledged as a Bond expert of unrivalled expertise.

You must introduce the subject carefully, though. Psycho-literary analysis of a fictional character and his derivation is fascinating, but launch straight into it when everyone else is talking about Roger Moore driving a car underwater and you'll sound like a nerd. A useful way to raise the topic is to mention one of 007's great paradoxes: the man billed as the world's most successful secret agent seems intent on 'preserving' that secrecy by announcing his surname to anyone who will listen, then repeating it (along with his first name) just in case they didn't catch it the first time.

When leading a conversation about Bond's character, you should always remember your central thesis: the books are better than the films. The most intriguing elements of Bond's character are those portrayed in the novels. Everyone else will be floundering in Sean Connery, Roger Moore, Pierce Brosnan and Daniel Craig; you can impress them with the man who created Bond: Ian Fleming. Who was his inspiration? The short answer (and a bluffer always values a short answer) seems to be Fleming himself.

BOND AS FLEMING (OR FLEMING AS BOND)

The similarities between author and creation are just too striking to ignore. A small selection will make the point for you:

* Both are the same height (6ft) and share the same eye colour (blue-grey).
* One of Fleming's mother's first names was St Croix; Bond's mother's maiden name was Delacroix.
* Both lost their fathers at an early age.
* Both went to Eton (although Bond was expelled in his first year).
* Both served in the Royal Naval Volunteer Reserve, rising from lieutenant to commander during the Second World War.
* Both smoked copiously. Fleming got through 70 a day, Bond 60–70, as in 'Bond lit his 34th cigarette

of the day. ...' And not just any old cigarettes, but ones made by Morland & Co. of Grosvenor Street with a specific mixture of Turkish and Balkan tobacco, decorated with three gold bands (to mirror a commander's stripes).

* Both Fleming and Bond carried a battered black oxidised Ronson lighter.
* Both wore a Rolex (although Fleming never specified which model).
* Both were partial to scrambled eggs and Béarnaise sauce.
* Bond fraternises at an exclusive and expensive club called Blades, based on Fleming's own club, Boodle's.
* Both had the same golf handicap (nine). You might well have expected Bond to be a scratch player; it's reassuring to know he has some imperfections.

One curious exception is that Fleming chose to share his own birthday, 28 May 1908, with Bond's arch-enemy, Blofeld. Perhaps we all dream of being a villain sometimes.

Fleming began writing the first Bond novel, *Casino Royale*, at the age of 43, as he was about to marry Ann Rothermere, the ex-wife of *Daily Mail* owner Viscount Rothermere. He claimed that Bond provided distraction from the horror of his impending marriage. It's little wonder, you can point out, that Bond's attitude towards women should draw so deeply on the personality of his creator.

Fleming wanted his hero to have 'the simplest, dullest, plainest-sounding name [he] could find.

"James Bond" was much better than something more interesting, like "Peregrine Maltravers".' The name was actually taken from an ornithological book, James Bond's *Field Guide to Birds of the West Indies*, that Ian Fleming kept at his Jamaican home. On no account, however, should you be tempted to make any of the obvious jokes about Bond and birds.

Why did Fleming want such a plain name? Because he envisaged Bond as a very human hero: 'a neutral figure – an anonymous blunt instrument wielded by a government department'. It's best to give your audience time to reflect on this fact. Men in particular will understand the concept of a blunt instrument, though in most cases it will be that chisel they keep meaning to replace.

Quite why Fleming chose '007' as Bond's Secret Service number has been the subject of considerable speculation over the years. Much of this has (as speculation is wont to do) strayed into the realms of the fanciful, with theories about the seven deadly sins, the seven virtues, the seven wonders of the world. ...

Some refer to the fact that, during the war, the Royal Navy used a 'double-0' prefix in its top-secret coded signals. However, you can go even further back and refer to mathematician John Dee, a favourite of Queen Elizabeth I, who was instructed to spy on King Philip II during her war against Spain. He marked his messages to her '007' – the seven denoting luck and the two zeros denoting eyes (as in 'for yours only'). There's no more evidence for this than for any of the other theories, but by quoting some history, you'll at least stand out.

BOND'S LOOKS

There's nothing better than going to the original source material. Hit your audience with this quote from *Casino Royale*:

> *It was a dark, clean-cut face, with a three-inch scar showing whitely down the sunburned skin of the right cheek. The eyes were wide and level under straight, rather long, black brows. The hair was black, parted on the left, and carelessly brushed so that a thick black comma fell down over the right eyebrow. The longish straight nose ran down to a short upper lip below which was a wide and finely drawn but cruel mouth.*

BOND'S CHARACTER

The best way of tackling James Bond's character is to concentrate on his essential unknowability. As Ian Fleming himself said:

> *The odd thing about Bond is that I didn't think of him as a 'character' at all. … He's a cipher, in fact. What's happened over the years is that he has become a 'character' largely exaggerated in the public mind. … He's a man of action primarily, and he's not a person of much social attractiveness. But then I never intended him to be a particularly likeable person. …*

BOND'S LIFESTYLE

Bond, like Fleming, is very particular in his tastes. The mass of detail Fleming used in the novels gives a real flavour of 007's world, especially the small luxuries with which he likes to surround himself. There's a strong notion of the comfort to be gained from old favourites, such as these:

* He wears Floris No 89 Eau de Toilette (the 89 comes from the number of the Floris shop in Jermyn Street, London). The citrus fragrance has shades of sandalwood, rose, orris and oakmoss.
* He washes his hair with Pinaud Elixir ('that prince among shampoos').
* He always wears 'dark blues and blacks and whites, the colours that betray an underlying melancholy'. His shirts are Sea Island cotton, his trousers worsted. He wears black silk knitted ties.
* His newspaper ('the only paper he ever read') is *The Times*.
* His only hobby is his car – a 4.5-litre Bentley coupé, which he drives 'hard and well and with an almost sensual pleasure' (*Casino Royale*).

When a man takes such care over his own comfort, it's easy to suspect that he's not really bothered about other people. Bond certainly seems to confirm this suspicion. In the end, he is always his own man, never giving too much of himself to others, and definitely not to women. One of the most famous passages about Bond's character (which you'd be well advised to memorise) appears in the first novel, *Casino Royale*:

> *The lengthy approaches to a seduction bored him almost as much as the subsequent mess of disentanglement. He found something grisly in the inevitability of the pattern of each affair. The conventional parabola – sentiment, the touch of the hand, the kiss, the passionate kiss, the feel of the body, the climax in bed, then more bed, then less bed, then the boredom, the tears, and the final bitterness – was to him shameful and hypocritical.*

It was just as well for his women that Bond avoided relationships with them. If any of them had moved in with him, they'd only have got into trouble for using his Pinaud Elixir.

BOND'S FOOD AND DRINK

Breakfast is Bond's favourite meal of the day. Given his 60-a-day smoking habit, you might expect him to consume a full English breakfast. Instead, when at home in his Chelsea flat, it is a solitary egg, cooked for three and a third minutes, followed by wholewheat toast with Jersey butter and a choice of Frank Cooper's Vintage Oxford Marmalade, Tiptree 'Little Scarlet' strawberry preserve or Norwegian heather honey from Fortnum & Mason, along with very strong coffee, *not tea*. Bond, to use his own word, 'hates' tea. In *Goldfinger,* a Secret Service canteen girl commits the heinous crime of bringing him a cup. He calls it 'mud', and cites it as a primary reason for the downfall of the British Empire.

While we're on the subject of eggs, Bond will eat one virtually any time, day or night, with or without orange juice, vodka and tonic, or champagne. A proofreader at Ian Fleming's publishing company was alarmed at how often 007 consumed scrambled eggs in an early draft of *Live and Let Die*; all an enemy would need do to track him is ask in each restaurant if a man had been there eating that particular dish.

In Bond's life, far more importance seems to be placed on the drink, rather than on the food that happens to accompany it.

The proofreader was too polite to mention another problem: how could Bond possibly complete his duties as a go-get-'em super-spy, given the effect so many eggs would have had on his digestion?

It gives fresh meaning to his response in *Octopussy* when, in pursuit of the fake Fabergé egg, Magda (*Octopussy*'s right-hand woman) says: 'He suggests a trade. The egg for your life.' And Bond replies: 'Well, I'd heard the price of eggs was going up, but isn't that a little high?'

Bond may well like the simple stuff, but insists that it is of the highest quality. Not just any eggs, but deep-brown eggs with a rich, yellow yolk laid by French hens of the Marans breed. Not just smoked salmon, but Scottish smoked salmon, cured in the Highlands. Sean Connery would have approved.

On the whole, unless in exotic locations, Bond is not that adventurous with food. In *Moonraker*, he and M dine together on asparagus with hollandaise sauce, then lamb cutlets with peas and new potatoes, followed by a plain slice of pineapple.

In Bond's life, far more importance seems to be placed on the drink, rather than on the food that happens to accompany it. For example, with caviar or smoked salmon he enjoys neat and ice-cold vodka, on top of which he drops a pinch of black pepper (which then sinks to the bottom) to rid the vodka of impurities – a trick he learned in Russia.

He is not averse to gin and tonic with Angostura bitters and the juice of fresh lime; bourbon (three fingers) in a tumbler half-filled with ice; or brandy and ginger on a long flight. But champagne is his favourite, whether Black Velvet (champagne and Guinness) alongside dressed crab, or rosé fizz with roast grouse.

In the film *Goldfinger*, Bond advises Jill Masterson that there are some things you just don't do, such as drinking Dom Pérignon 1953 above 38° Fahrenheit. It's a great detail, but if you ever find yourself repeating it without your tongue firmly in your cheek, you might as well get your coat and leave immediately. And although he likes Dom Pérignon and Veuve Clicquot, Bond's real label of choice is Taittinger.

In truth, there really isn't much that Bond *won't* drink (apart from tea). During the course of *On Her Majesty's Secret Service* (the book), he manages to down an impressive 46 drinks, including wine, champagne (Taittinger, naturally), whisky, bourbon, vodka, brandy, schnapps, gin, and four full *steins* of German beer. Miraculously, none of this appears to impair his ability to drive or operate machinery.

Bond's most famous idiosyncrasy, of course, is his preference as to how a vodka martini should be served. But why? Bond orders his martini this way in chapter nine of *Diamonds Are Forever*, but gives no reason for it. You can have fun with the following reasons suggested by others:

1. Shaking the drink dilutes it and enables Bond to keep a clear head.

2. The shaken version contains stronger antioxidant properties that remove harmful substances from the blood and body.

3. The explanation Ian Fleming gave in real life: shaking the drink makes it colder.

Should you find yourself forgetting any of these, you can fall back on the line used by Daniel Craig in his first outing as Bond (*Casino Royale*, 2006). To show that the new actor would be departing from his predecessors' portrayals, when Craig is asked whether he would like his martini shaken or stirred he replies: 'Do I look like I give a damn?'

Bond's recipe for the martini, known as the 'Vesper', is given in *Casino Royale* (the book, not the film). In this highly potent formula, you mix gin with vodka, and a splash of Lillet Blanc,* an aromatic apéritif with a dark undertone of orange, made in the French town of Podensac. It could be a nifty gambit to purchase a bottle and offer the cocktail to guests while quoting Bond's own words: 'Three measures of Gordon's, one of vodka, half a measure of Kina Lillet,* shake it very well until it's ice-cold, then add a large, thin slice of lemon peel.'

* Pronounced *lee-lay*. *Kina* was its original name. According to Kingsley Amis, Fleming made an error with this martini because the quinine content (now reduced) in this fortified wine would have made the mixture far too bitter to enjoy.

Whenever James Bond gets mentioned at any social gathering, you can guarantee that within a few seconds everyone will be discussing who was better, Sean Connery or Roger Moore.

INSPIRATION AND PORTRAYAL

BOND AS OTHERS

As much as Ian Fleming gave James Bond his own habits and characteristics, the sad truth (from Fleming's point of view) is that when it came to what matters – the missions, the spying, the killing – his novels were nothing more than wish fulfilment. Fleming served in Naval Intelligence during the Second World War, and helped supervise the 1940 escape from France of refugees fleeing the advancing Nazis. Whether or not he progressed further than a desk in Whitehall is disputed.

If he didn't, it wasn't for want of trying. He constantly dreamed up ambitious (not to say hazardous) schemes for defeating the Germans, with the intention of taking part himself. One, which Fleming dubbed 'Operation Goldeneye', was a plan for the defence of Gibraltar.

Another, called 'Operation Ruthless', was designed to capture German naval Enigma machine codebooks. Fleming and his co-agents were to have dressed in German air force uniforms, complete with bandages soaked in fake blood, then to have crashed a captured enemy plane into the sea, near the ship carrying the Enigma documentation. When rescued, they were to have overpowered the Germans, taken control of the ship and sailed it back to Britain. Unsurprisingly, the scheme was never given the go-ahead. But it's clear that a man who could come up with ideas like this was never going to end up writing books on gardening.

A successful venture in which Fleming did play a part was 'Operation Mincemeat', the plot to plant a dead body bearing false intelligence about Allied landings (later portrayed in the film *The Man Who Never Was*) and allow it to wash up in mainland Europe. He also helped set up America's Office of Strategic Services, which ultimately became the CIA, and for which he was given a revolver engraved with the words: 'For Special Services'.

Fleming oversaw a team of crack soldiers who were known as '30 AU' ('Assault Unit'), which he referred to as his 'Red Indians'. Seconded from the regular army, these likely lads were given specialist training in Bond-ish activities such as safe-cracking and unarmed combat, then dispatched overseas on intelligence-gathering and sabotage missions. It's from this unit that you can draw the first of your possible 'Bond prototypes'. The following are just some of the men who are commonly thought to have inspired Fleming as he was fleshing out his fictional character:

Michael Mason (Sadly, no relation to this book's author). A member of the landed gentry, he turned his back on cucumber sandwiches and cocktails at The Ritz to become a successful boxer, then a trapper in Canada. He once sailed six cement barges up the River Danube in an attempt to block it and hinder the Nazis. He failed, but escaped the Germans' clutches.

Commander Wilfred Dunderdale The Secret Intelligence Service's station chief in Paris. He funded his spying escapades from his own fortune, wore Cartier cufflinks and drove around in a bulletproof Rolls-Royce. All of which are good reasons for mentioning him – but not as good as the best reason of all, which is that he was known as 'Biffy'.

Lieutenant Commander Patrick Dalzel-Job A colleague of Fleming's in Naval Intelligence. He could ski backwards and navigate a midget submarine (though not at the same time), and disobeyed orders by rescuing the women and children of Narvik, Norway, from the Germans during the Second World War. He was saved from a court martial only by the King of Norway's intervention. Fleming confirmed that Dalzel-Job had been in his thoughts as he created Bond, but the man himself shunned the stories as 'far too dramatic'. Which is itself Bond-like.

Sir William Stephenson British intelligence chief in North America during the Second World War, code name 'Intrepid'. He scores points for that, though not as many as for Fleming's quote that 'James Bond is a highly romanticised version of a true spy. The real thing is William Stephenson.' But Fleming was (not for the first time) being a little playful; no one man was really the basis for 007, except possibly …

Lieutenant Colonel Geoffrey Gordon-Creed A former Downside public schoolboy, he won the Military Cross for extraordinary valour in his first action, aged 21. Gordon-Creed was an ex-tank commander recruited by the Special Operations Executive to disrupt German supply lines in wartime Greece. A serial seducer of equally heroic proportions, later adding Ava Gardner to his long list of lovers, and the daughter of the president of Firestone (then one of the world's wealthiest companies) to his long list of wives, the highly decorated soldier's guerrilla activities in occupied Greece would have been well known to Fleming – not least when he added the Distinguished Service Order (DSO) to his medal haul.

Cruelly handsome, and never happier than when dispatching an enemy with a knife or pouncing on any female within sight, the man who has since been described as a 'lethal weapon' was a drinking companion of Fleming's in Jamaica in the early 1950s. His biographer, Falklands veteran Roger Field, has no doubts that Gordon-Creed was the true inspiration for Bond. The other stuffed shirts simply didn't place enough emphasis on the importance of sex.

WHO WAS THE FIRST BOND?

So comprehensively has James Bond been taken over by the James Bond movies that many people think the whole thing started with Sean Connery. It's understandable that an actor who rhymes 'yes' with 'mesh' should capture everybody's attention, but as a bluffer, you pride yourself on not being everybody. You go the extra mile; you take the extra step; you read the extra paragraph. Then, when others have finished, you quietly mention that Connery was not, in fact, the first actor to play James Bond – and the floor is yours.

The late Bob Holness, who famously didn't play the saxophone solo on Gerry Rafferty's 'Baker Street' (despite an urban myth that he did), and who ultimately ended up as the host of the TV quiz *Blockbusters*, played Bond in a 1956 South African radio adaptation of *Moonraker*. But even he wasn't the first 007. On 21 October 1954, a year after the publication of *Casino Royale*, James Bond finally sprang from the pages. The first man to play him was American actor Barry Nelson, in a one-hour TV play that formed part of the CBS network's *Climax!* series, later known as *Climax Mystery Theater*.

Unfortunately, what should have been a momentous cultural event was spoiled for Bond purists by a number of factors:

* The character was Americanised as 'Jimmy Bond' (the idea of anyone calling Bond 'Jimmy' is unimaginable).
* In the book, Vesper Lynd, the double agent with whom Bond has fallen in love, kills herself. His contradictory emotions – despair at losing the one he loves, anger at her deception – help provide the darkness, subtlety and depth that fans of the books appreciate. In this US TV version, Lynd is renamed Valerie Mathis, and does not kill herself. But since when did American TV producers worry about accuracy?

*   The play was transmitted live, which is always rather dangerous. Something went wrong with the timings, because the viewers at home saw Peter Lorre (who played villain Le Chiffre) get up after being 'killed' and jauntily return to his dressing room.

Should you wish to progress to an extra level of bluffing, you can reveal that Barry Nelson went on to appear in *The Shining*. He plays the manager of the Overlook Hotel, who runs Jack Nicholson through the duties that will be expected of him as caretaker over the winter.

WHO WAS THE BEST BOND?

Whenever James Bond gets mentioned at any social gathering, you can guarantee that within a few seconds everyone will be discussing who was better, Sean Connery or Roger Moore. Naturally, 90% of people will prefer Sean Connery. For many of the women (and one or two of the men), this opinion will be based purely on looks. It's hard to deny that Connery possessed an aura of convincing danger that Moore simply couldn't match, while in his later Bond outings, the massive amounts of hair on Connery's chest seem to have distracted people from the 'interesting' hair on his head.

There is no question, however, which actor wins the prize for the most apposite name for playing the role of 007. If you didn't know that 'Roger Moore' was, in fact, Rog's birth name, you'd swear that he'd adopted it as a pseudonym to hint at a tendency towards sexual profligacy.

Bluffers will, of course, be expected to pass judgement on the best Bond. Initially you should opt for one of the three actors who ignore cheesiness in order to bring an edge to the role, closer to Ian Fleming's original vision: George Lazenby, Timothy Dalton or Daniel Craig. This approach will lend you the credibility that always clings to people who read books rather than watch films. Lazenby, for instance, is the preferred choice of many Bond aficionados who otherwise prefer to stick to the novels.

In his later Bond outings, the massive amounts of hair on Connery's chest seem to have distracted people from the 'interesting' hair on his head.

If you plump for Dalton, you should refer to the fact that the actor cited *Casino Royale* as his own favourite 007 novel, on account of Bond's 'moral and ethical confusion'. People tend to be impressed by phrases like this.

It's pretty easy to argue the case for Craig: battered good looks, eyes like a shark, a cruel mouth, the skilful rendering of Bond's darker character traits, etc. And of course, those tackle-defining swimming trunks.

Pierce Brosnan, mind you, is a useful fallback position. Unequivocally handsome, he is also Irish – and after a Scotsman (Connery), an Englishman (Moore), and a Welshman (Dalton), it was an Irishman's turn. Certainly with *GoldenEye* he helped restore faith in the

Bond genre at a time when many had written it off, arguing that, with the fall of the Berlin Wall and the Soviet Union's collapse, 007's work was done. If you wish to add weight to this opinion, you can reveal that Brosnan had in fact been offered the role of Bond once before, when Roger Moore retired, but because of a commitment to the TV series *Remington Steele*, he'd had to refuse. This must have been like turning down a Rolls-Royce because you'd paid the deposit on a Skoda.

But however much you protest that you're un-interested in the Connery/Moore debate, you will inevitably get dragged into it. Tempting as it is to side with the majority view – if for no other reason than Connery's first four films are those that bear the closest resemblance to the books on which they're based – there's a lot to be said for playing devil's advocate. Even if you can't muster the courage to say 'Moore was better' out loud, the following points can be mentioned in Roger's defence:

1. It's human nature to prefer an original to its copy. Connery had the chance to imprint himself on the world's imagination as the definitive Bond. If Moore had been given that chance, cinema-goers might well be sitting around mocking the vulgar Scotsman who came along in his wake. Moore himself was aware of this danger; in none of his films did he ever order a 'vodka martini, shaken not shtirred', precisely because it would lead to accusations of imitating Connery.

2. Ian Fleming himself wanted Roger Moore to play Bond. When the producers were casting the first film,

Dr No, Fleming initially suggested his friend David Niven (though Sean Connery is on record as recalling that Fleming 'always wanted Cary Grant to play the role, but he was unaffordable'). After it was pointed out that Niven was too old, Fleming opted for Moore, who was then playing *The Saint* on TV.

3. Fleming had severe doubts about Harry Saltzman's choice of Sean Connery, wondering how a working-class Scot with a lisp could possibly play his public-school-educated hero. He only relented after lunch with Connery at The Savoy, where another guest, the Marchioness of Milford Haven, assured Fleming that Connery had 'it'. As James Bond gets quite a bit of 'it', this was important.

4. Most of Connery's Bond outings were in the 1960s; most of Moore's were in the 1970s. How could Connery fail to win? He was operating during the coolest decade in history, the era of the Beatles, JFK and the Apollo Moon landings. All Moore had for a backdrop was loons and Showaddywaddy. And the less said about his powder-blue safari suit, the better.

5. Moore never took himself too seriously. He once commented on Twitter about a journalist's references to 'my silly renditions as 007. Fair enough, I thought, on my Monte-Carlo balcony.'

But the best way to win people over to Moore is to recount the anecdote shared by Mark Haynes, a scriptwriter from London. As a seven-year-old in 1983, Haynes was flying with his grandfather from Nice airport. Seeing Roger Moore at the departure gate, the young boy asked for an autograph. Moore duly signed his name. As he and his grandfather walked away, Haynes looked at the signature and became confused. Why did it not read 'James Bond'? His grandfather returned to the star, and explained the situation. Moore's face 'crinkled up' in realisation, and he beckoned the boy over. Looking from side to side, he whispered: 'I have to sign my name as "Roger Moore" because otherwise. ... Blofeld might find out I was here.' Haynes instantly became thrilled that James Bond had entrusted him with his secret.

Two decades later, Haynes was working on a UNICEF film for which Moore was recording a piece to camera. Haynes told him the story about Nice airport. Moore chuckled, and said: 'Well, I don't remember but I'm glad you got to meet James Bond.' Then he delivered his lines. After the filming, as he was leaving, Moore paused next to Haynes and looked both ways. He murmured: 'Of course I remember our meeting in Nice. But I didn't say anything in there, because those cameramen – any one of them could be working for Blofeld.' As Haynes says: 'I was as delighted at 30 as I had been at 7. What a tremendous man.'

WHO WAS BOND, WHEN?
Sean Connery 1962–67
Dr No (1962)
From Russia with Love (1963)
Goldfinger (1964)
Thunderball (1965)
You Only Live Twice (1967)

George Lazenby 1969
On Her Majesty's Secret Service (1969)

....

Sean Connery* 1971
Diamonds Are Forever (1971)

....

Roger Moore 1973–85
Live and Let Die (1973)
The Man with the Golden Gun (1974)
The Spy Who Loved Me (1977)
Moonraker (1979)
For Your Eyes Only (1981)
Octopussy (1983)
A View to a Kill (1985)

....

Sean Connery** 1983
Never Say Never Again (1983)

....

Timothy Dalton 1987–89
The Living Daylights (1987)
Licence to Kill (1989)

....

The Dark Age – No Bond 1989–95

....

Pierce Brosnan 1995–2002
GoldenEye (1995)
Tomorrow Never Dies (1997)
The World Is Not Enough (1999)
Die Another Day (2002)

* Comeback number one
** Comeback number two

Daniel Craig 2006–
Casino Royale (2006)
Quantum of Solace (2008)
Skyfall (2012)
Spectre (2015)
No Time To Die (2020).

THE BOOKS VS. THE FILMS

THE BOOKS

The key to bluffing your way in Bond is to understand one crucial fact: the films are nowhere near as good as the books – even when Fleming was noticeably losing his touch towards the end. Once you have adopted this as your central argument, everything you say will earn the respect due an obvious expert.

Most Bond aficionados rate Ian Fleming's novels about the spy significantly above the much more famous films. If you do the same, you'll benefit, whatever the situation, for one of the following two main reasons:

1. Even when your audience is aware of the books, it will be pretty unusual for them to have read any (especially if they're under 40). If you show that you're familiar with the novels, you'll convince others that you really do know what you're on about. Everything you say about Bond, even when discussing the inferior film version, will be listened to with open-mouthed admiration.

2. A large number of people don't know that the books exist (depressing, but true). To such an audience, your pronouncements might as well be written on tablets of stone.

Serious Bond fans prefer the books to the films for reasons that tend to centre on the character of Bond himself. Fleming painted a portrait of a dark, complex man, very much a loner, rarely troubled by conscience, with tendencies towards misogyny. With very few exceptions, the films present Bond as a one-dimensional cartoon hero addicted to flashy gadgets, whose most taxing moral choice is whether he should (a) blow up the volcano then bed the girl in the bikini, or (b) bed the girl in the bikini then blow up the volcano.

When you're trying to persuade people of the books' superiority over the films ... use the phrase 'moral complexity' a lot. It tends to impress.

When you're trying to persuade people of the books' superiority over the films, it's best that you concentrate on the nature of Bond's character. Use the phrase 'moral complexity' a lot. It tends to impress, and will have them thinking you're some sort of Melvyn Bragg. They'll be cautious about arguing with you for fear of appearing shallow; instead, with luck, they'll just nod contemplatively and bow to your superior knowledge. If any of them do threaten to step out of line, all you have to do is quote a line or two from one of the books to illustrate your point. It's well worth committing a couple of these examples to memory.

It was part of his profession to kill people. He had never liked doing it and when he had to kill he did it as well as he knew how and forgot about it. As a secret agent who held the rare double-0 prefix – the licence to kill in the Secret Service – it was his duty to be as cool about death as a surgeon. If it happened, it happened. Regret was unprofessional – worse, it was a death-watch beetle in the soul.
Goldfinger

It was one of those days when it seemed to James Bond that all life, as someone put it, was nothing but a heap of six to four against.
Thunderball

The blubbery arms of the soft life had Bond round the neck and they were slowly strangling him. He was a man of war, and when, for a long period, there was no war, his spirit went into a decline.
From Russia with Love

James Bond, with two double bourbons inside him, sat in the final departure lounge of Miami Airport and thought about life and death.
Goldfinger

Then, as gently as you can, ask your opponent how he or she can possibly defend a series of films in which 'emotional depth' translates as Roger Moore raising an eyebrow. If this fails to convince, use the ultimate argument for the books being better than the films: namely that the film-makers themselves decided to return to the novels for inspiration when choosing a successor to Pierce Brosnan.

It was explicitly stated that in casting Daniel Craig and in downplaying 007's gadgets to produce a 'darker' film, the producers wanted 2006's *Casino Royale* to mark a return to the 'true' Bond. They were so sure that this was the right move that they announced Craig's rehiring for a further film before the shooting of *Casino Royale* had even finished. Praise indeed. Not even Bond himself got his next job before finishing the one he was working on at the time.

You should then put forward the theory that the producers reduced the role of gadgetry because everyday technology had improved so much in recent years that it was becoming harder and harder to impress the average moviegoer. For instance, in *Goldfinger*, 007 tracks the villain's car by means of a crude buzzing device that doesn't even give the car's exact location, just how near it is. Today, even the most basic sat-nav system from Argos can do more than that.

As recently as Pierce Brosnan's tenure, Bond audiences were wowed by Secret Service computers in which you could instantly view any location in the world via satellite, simply by tapping in a place name, a postcode or a grid reference. These days, it's called Google Earth.

If even that fails to silence your tech-obsessed opponent, put him (and inevitably, it will be a him) in the spare room with your child's Nintendo Switch. The rest of you can then get on with a proper conversation about the superiority of the Bond books.

THE FILMS

By the early 1960s, Bond's exploits on the page had guaranteed him a welcome on the big screen. The big issue was who would take him there. Step forward American producer Cubby Broccoli, whose real first name was Albert, but who received the nickname as a child after a cartoon character of the time. He once made the claim that one of his ancestors had invented broccoli by crossing a cauliflower with a particular sort of lettuce. Whether this is true or not, we can't say. He was a movie producer, after all.

Broccoli discovered that the film rights to Bond had been optioned by Canadian producer Harry Saltzman in 1961. Saltzman was a born showman, who by the age of 15 was touring Europe as manager of a travelling circus. He didn't mind that the elephants were hugely expensive to feed and transport – they were what the public wanted to see. He took the same approach to movies: 'Give the public what they want. Give them elephants. Put everything up there on the screen. The bigger, the better.'

Cubby and Harry teamed up and, as their enterprise was such a risk, they called the company EON Productions – 'Everything Or Nothing'. In the event, it was the former. Since 1962, the Bond movies have grossed something in the region of $6 billion (£3.7 billion). Even SPECTRE only dared ask for £100 million. It wasn't just the films themselves that made EON rich – there was the merchandising too. By 1972 the franchise had given rise to no fewer than 250 licensed products in 70 countries. There was 007 vodka, there was 007 aftershave, there was 007 everything.

As the revenues grew, so did the budgets for the films. Saltzman always wanted more explosions, more car chases, more excess in general. 'What are you worrying about?' went his catchphrase. 'It's only money!'

But the profligacy did not extend to the actors' wage bills. Saltzman allegedly paid extras with cash from a suitcase, which may seem appropriately Bondish, but was actually done to avoid the tax liabilities that would have arisen from having registered employees. Even Sean Connery experienced the producers' parsimony. They stubbornly refused to renegotiate his flat-fee contract and give him a share of the profits. Believing he should be their partner on equal terms, Connery came to develop a pathological dislike of Broccoli and Saltzman. He even refused to work if they visited the set.

The pair's luxurious offices in Mayfair had several Bond villain touches – Turkish bath, private cinema furnished in red leather – but so, in the end, did their relationship. Saltzman insisted on making other films on his own, and when these failed he ended up with debts of $20 million. By 1975 he was forced to sell out to Broccoli. There were lawsuits, there was ill-feeling. The pair parted without shaking hands or saying goodbye.

Broccoli once claimed that half the world's population had seen a Bond film. While this may be another moment to remind your audience that he was a movie producer, you can nevertheless assume that most of them will have seen at least one of them. Consequently, there is very little bluffing value to be gained from knowing the plots, which, apart from the first few films, bear little or no relation to the relevant books.

In each case, we recommend a one-line summary to help your audience differentiate the film from its stablemates, then a snippet or two of 'behind the scenes' trivia to show your superior knowledge. Being able to bluff even about films you don't like will show a truly impressive command of your subject.

Most Bond fans know about Roger Moore wrestling on top of a cable car in **Moonraker** *the film, but tell them what actually happened in* **Moonraker** *the book and you'll really capture their attention.*

EARLY DAYS

In the space of 11 years, Fleming wrote 12 Bond novels and two collections of Bond short stories, the final books being published after his death. It is crucial that you know something about these, even if it's only a little something.

Because your whole proposition, after all, is that the books are in a different league to the films, you should be able to show at least some familiarity with them. Most Bond fans know about Roger Moore wrestling on top of a cable car in *Moonraker* the film, but tell them what actually happened in *Moonraker* the book and you'll really capture their attention. For example, the megalomaniac Hugo Drax is a former high-ranking Nazi whose sidekick Krebbs shares the same name as Hitler's last chief of staff.

Comparing and contrasting the books and the films will offer you 'MBV', or Maximum Bluffing Value. Even if you remember nothing else, just memorise these nuggets of interest, and you will prevail over anybody who dares to question your Bond expertise.

So, as Q always said when he was demonstrating to Bond the gadgets for his next adventure, 'Pay attention.'

CASINO ROYALE
The Book (1953)
In this first of the Bond novels, Bond defeats Le Chiffre (a French union leader who is actually a Russian double agent) at cards in order to bankrupt him. Le Chiffre then kidnaps Vesper Lynd, a beautiful MI6 agent loaned to Bond as a personal assistant; 007 tries to rescue her, but is captured and tortured. An assassin from SMERSH, the Soviet agency Le Chiffre double-crossed, kills Le Chiffre but spares Bond. Lynd herself turns out to be a double-agent, knows her Russian masters are on to her and commits suicide.

Memorable scene Le Chiffre ties Bond to a bottomless chair then repeatedly strikes his unprotected undercarriage with a carpet beater. Unconventional as torture goes, but undeniably effective. Watch the male members of your audience wince when you mention this.

Reaction The debut Bond novel sold well without becoming a runaway success. The critics liked it, calling it 'thoroughly exciting'. An exception was writer Hugo Charteris, who called the book 'neurotic' and 'disgusting'. This must have been particularly irksome for Fleming – Charteris was his brother-in-law.

MBV 'Vesper' was taken from a rum cocktail Fleming encountered on his first trip to Jamaica. In the book, Bond gives the name to another cocktail – a martini containing both gin and vodka – as a tribute to Vesper Lynd. Like his famous vodka martini, he takes it shaken, not stirred.

The Films (1967 and 2006)

Casino Royale is the only Bond novel that has been adapted twice for the screen.

The 1967 version starred David Niven as 'Sir James Bond', Woody Allen as 'Dr Noah', Orson Welles as Le Chiffre, John Huston as M, and Peter Sellers as ... actually nobody was quite sure who Sellers was, least of all Sellers himself. The film was variously described as a spoof, a comedy, and also possibly a satire. It has also been described as one of the truly great bad movies of all time, so you can safely call it a cinematic car crash. Amazingly, most of the cast emerged from the wreckage with their reputations relatively undamaged – unlike the six directors in the credits (who included Val Guest, the man who went on to direct the seminal *Confessions of a Window Cleaner*). By far the best thing about the film was Dusty Springfield's smoky soundtrack rendition of 'The Look of Love'.

The *Casino Royale* film version you really need to know about is the 2006 movie that introduced Daniel Craig as the new Bond. Critics were almost unanimous in acknowledging that he came closer to capturing the cold ruthlessness of the trained killer of the novels than any actor since Sean Connery. The producers' intent to get serious, almost certainly to compete with *The Bourne Trilogy*, was signalled by the fact that this was the first movie since *Dr No* not to feature naked silhouettes of dancing women in the opening title sequence. And they included the testicle-thrashing scene, which couldn't have been an easy decision.

Trivia Craig took his new role seriously; he even gave up smoking to get into shape. All this from such a whippersnapper; he's the first Bond actor to have come into the world *after* the film series itself started. Born in 1968, he is younger than the first five movies. Other actors considered for the part of 007 included Hugh Jackman, Clive Owen, Dougray Scott and James Purefoy. Craig reportedly landed the role after Barbara Broccoli (Cubby's daughter) saw him in the 2004 cult film *Layer Cake*.

Noted self-publicist Sir Richard Branson has a cameo role, and a Virgin Atlantic plane is shown in the airport scene. However, in the in-flight version shown by British Airways, Branson's appearance was cut and the logos on the Virgin Atlantic plane were blurred out. That's product displacement for you.

Faithfulness to the novel 8/10.

Dare say 'I do wish Craig wouldn't affect such a ridiculous pout. And those bright-blue contact lenses are absurd, even if they do match his budgie smugglers.'

Do speculate 'For an experienced former naval officer, Bond wasn't much cop at giving CPR in the drowning scene. With a bit more application, Vesper might have come round.'

LIVE AND LET DIE
The Book (1954)

Bond is sent to New York to investigate Mr Big (New York seems to be full of them), a voodoo baron suspected of smuggling gold to fund Soviet activity in America. Because Mr Big works for SMERSH, Bond can't resist the opportunity to rescue the criminal's unwilling girlfriend, Solitaire, with whom he travels to Florida, then Jamaica.

Next, Bond swims underwater to Mr Big's private island, where he fixes a limpet mine to Mr Big's boat before being captured. Solitaire has already been caught again, and Mr Big is about to kill them both by dragging them behind his boat over a coral reef when the mine explodes and the injured villain's blood attracts a shark attack. Spielberg, eat your heart out.

Memorable scene Bond and his CIA ally, Felix Leiter, visit Mr Big's Harlem club, The Boneyard, where a beautiful dancer, G-G Sumatra, performs a sexually charged striptease to the accompaniment of voodoo drummers.

Intent Fleming wanted the book (originally titled *The Undertaker's Wind*) to be more serious than its predecessor, delving deeper into the nature of evil and taking up themes that *Casino Royale* had only touched on. But he got caught up in the fast action and vivid descriptions and lost some of his original intent.

Nevertheless, there are moments when Mr Big muses on the criminal psyche, explaining that it arises from spiritual lethargy (what early Christians called 'accidie'). Mention this after dinner. The idea that sluggishness leads to all the bad in the world is an interesting one to raise when people are sitting there with a stomach full of sticky toffee pudding.

MBV Fleming sent a copy to Winston Churchill, calling it 'an unashamed thriller … its only merit is that it makes no demands on the mind of the reader'. Incidentally, he always carried with him *The Times* obituary that Churchill had written for his father, Valentine Fleming, who was killed in the First World War, eight days before his son's ninth birthday.

The Film (1973)
This is the one where Roger Moore, in his first outing as Bond, runs across the alligators. His stuntman had an uncomfortable moment when the last alligator snapped at his leg, ripping his fashionably flared trousers.

Trivia Whenever something went wrong during filming, the crew would apparently shout out 'Send for Sean!' – or 'Shend for Sean!' if they were feeling particularly witty. Sir Paul McCartney provided the theme song, although he credited his wife Linda with writing the reggae-style middle section. Having flown to the film set in Jamaica to play the finished recording to the producers, McCartney was reportedly a little put-out to be told: 'That's great for a demo. When can you get the proper version done?' Then, of course, there is the best opportunity for outwitting grammar pedants ever afforded by a popular song. They think McCartney is singing: 'And if this ever-changing world in which we live in', so they criticise him for the repetition. But Macca's lyric is actually: 'And if this ever-changing world in which we're living.' Wait for them to pontificate, then quietly put them in their place. Mind you, the fact we're talking about three syllables from the soundtrack tells you all you need to know about the film itself.

Faithfulness to the novel 3/10.

Do ask 'Was Roger Moore channelling an embryonic Austin Powers?'
Dare say 'This is the worst Bond soundtrack by some distance, and that includes A-ha's "The Living Daylights".'

MOONRAKER
The Book (1955)
This is the only Bond novel to be set exclusively in England. It starts in London with Bond exposing noted industrialist Sir Hugo Drax for cheating at cards. He then follows Drax to Kent, where the villain has developed the Moonraker rocket, offering to donate it to Britain's defence.

Working with the beautiful Gala Brand, a member of Drax's team (though in fact an undercover policewoman), Bond discovers that the rocket is aimed at London, and that Drax is an agent of SMERSH. Drax traps them inside the launch pad (the site is cut into the cliffs), but Gala and Bond manage to reset the coordinates so that the rocket lands in the sea, killing Drax. Bond expects to get the girl, but she's due to marry someone else. It's comforting to know that 007 gets the occasional knockback too.

Memorable scene The 62-page side story involving a game of bridge, set in the fictional London gentlemen's club Blades, in which Bond reveals Drax's system for cheating.

Drugs In the movies, Bond never consumes anything stronger than cigarettes or martinis. But Fleming went a stage further in this book: to keep his wits about him for the long card game, Bond mixes the stimulant Benzedrine into his champagne. No toilet cubicle and rolled-up banknote for 007; even the way he takes his drugs is stylish.

MBV An early title for the novel was *Mondays Are Hell*. Most people would agree with that statement.

The Film (1979)
This is the one where Rog and Jaws, the over-the-top villain, wrestle on top of a cable car on Sugarloaf Mountain, Rio de Janeiro. Movie buffs will know that the definitive cable-car fight scene had already been done in the 1968 film *Where Eagles Dare*, and that the fight didn't happen in the novel (like most of the rest of the film's storyline.) Gala Brand doesn't make an appearance, and is replaced by the raunchily named Holly Goodhead.

Trivia *For Your Eyes Only* had been planned as the next Bond film, but the producers switched to *Moonraker* to cash in on the success of the sci-fi boom started by *Star Wars*.

The keypad code unlocking the villain's laboratory plays the theme from *Close Encounters of the Third Kind*.

The steel cable which Jaws bites into in the aerial fight scene was actually made of liquorice.

Faithfulness to the novel 1/10.

Dare say 'Holly Goodhead is arguably one of the most suggestively named of all the Bond girls.'
Don't say 'But it's really not quite as suggestive as the name "Roger Moore".'

DIAMONDS ARE FOREVER
The Book (1956)
Bond infiltrates a diamond-smuggling ring run by twin brothers Jack and Seraffimo Spang, leaders of the Spangled Mob. Teaming up with Tiffany Case, a beautiful blonde member of the gang, he tracks them to Saratoga Springs, New York, where they try to fix a horse race before moving on to Las Vegas. Here Bond's cover is exposed, and Seraffimo's henchmen Wint and Kidd beat him up. He and Tiffany escape, killing Seraffimo by derailing his train.

They sail back to London on the *Queen Elizabeth*; Wint and Kidd, also on board, capture Tiffany, but Bond rescues her and kills them. Bond then travels to French Guinea, the source of the smuggled diamonds, where he kills Jack Spang by shooting down his helicopter.

Memorable scene Bond diverts Seraffimo's train (*The Cannonball*) at high speed on to a branch line leading into a disused mine shaft. This appears to be relatively straightforward, but in getting the right locomotive on the right track at the right time, Bond achieves something many rail companies in Britain can't manage.

Marriage The novel reveals more of Bond's ambivalent attitude towards women. While undeniably captivated by them, he nonetheless fears commitment. Tiffany tells him that people can't be complete by themselves. Bond, however, sees marriage not as adding two people together but subtracting one from the other. You might suggest that it's a good thing he went into espionage rather than relationship counselling.

MBV As research for the Las Vegas scenes, Fleming and his friend Ernie Cuneo played blackjack. As soon as they were a dollar up (not a huge sum even in the 1950s), they moved to the next casino. Repeating this procedure all night, they were soon boasting that they had 'taken on every casino in Vegas and won'.

The Film (1971)
This is the one where Bond nearly gets incinerated in a coffin. Jill St John stars as the first red-headed Bond girl (although she wears a blonde wig at one point), and English actor Charles Gray is the definitively urbane Blofeld.

Trivia Connery was tempted back to the role he'd come to loathe by the not-untempting matter of £1.2 million, at the time the highest fee ever received by any film star, and certainly more than he might have been paid in his earlier career as an Edinburgh milkman. He used most of the money to found the Scottish International Education Trust to give grants to young people and enterprising ventures in Scotland. This in spite of a reputation for being one of the meanest movie stars in the game.

The film contains what has to be the worst continuity error in the film franchise's history. Connery flips his car on to its right-hand wheels to drive through a narrow alley. When it emerges at the other end, however, the car is on its left-hand wheels. The producers realised the mistake in time, so filmed an insertion shot in which Connery deliberately re-flips the car. How is that possible in such a narrow space? If you ever need to argue against Bond movies as the height of skilled production, this will be your clincher.

Useful bluffing note Charles Gray was a contemporary of Benny Hill at school in Bournemouth.

Faithfulness to the novel 4/10.

Dare say 'Charles Gray was an absolute natural with a pussy on his lap. Strange. He was rumoured to be as camp as a row of pink tents.'
Dare ask 'Was this the film in which Sean had more hair in his eyebrows than under his hairpiece?'

FROM RUSSIA WITH LOVE
The Book (1957)

Russian agent Tatiana Romanova wants to defect because she has fallen in love with a picture of Bond in a KGB file. Yes, he's that good-looking. He is lured to Istanbul by a SMERSH plot concocted by the lesbian KGB colonel, Rosa Klebb. Surviving several attempts on his life, 007 (aided by the Turk Darko Kerim) brings Tatiana and her Spektor coding machine back to Paris on the *Orient Express*. En route, Kerim is killed by Russian agents, and Bond has to rescue Tatiana from SMERSH operative Red Grant, an ex-IRA member (not an easy opponent, but Bond kills him). In Paris, Rosa Klebb herself tries to kill Bond. She is captured, but not before she can kick out at him with a poison-tipped knife concealed in her boot. The novel ends with Bond collapsing on to the floor.

Memorable scene In Istanbul, Kerim takes Bond to witness a fight between two gypsy girls, who end up naked and sweating.

Ennui This, the fifth Bond book, is the favourite for many serious fans. Having said that, it was the first in which Fleming started to feel bored with his hero. He wrote to Philip Marlowe's creator, Raymond Chandler, that it was becoming harder to make Bond 'go through his tawdry tricks'.

This was part of a wider disenchantment with life itself:

while writing the novel, Fleming read (and identified with) F. Scott Fitzgerald's account of his nervous breakdown, *The Crack-Up*. At 48, Fleming feared he was 'too old to cut the mustard'. The novel's ambiguous end gave him the option of killing Bond off. By publication, however, his confidence was back. Worried correspondents received a reply saying a bulletin had been posted on the canteen noticeboard at Secret Service HQ: Bond was recovering.

MBV The scene in which Bond makes love to Tatiana aboard the *Orient Express* was based on a pre-war trip to Europe during which Fleming and a married actress wiled away a night aboard a wagon-lit. Research – it's such a drag.

The Film (1963)

This is the one with the really convincing fight scene in the train compartment. It was no secret that off camera the two protagonists, Connery and Robert Shaw, weren't the best of friends – and it showed. Many Bond aficionados rate this as the best of the franchise, capturing the atmosphere of cold war menace better than any other film of the Sixties (with the possible exception of *The Ipcress File*). Fewer gadgets, fewer gimmicks, no evil megalomaniacs; just a tense, tight production with plenty of suspense. Connery rated it as his favourite.

Trivia The legendary 'gun barrel' opening – Bond is framed in an assassin's sights, then turns to shoot, covering the screen in blood – was filmed by a stuntman rather than Sean Connery, who didn't film this sequence himself until *Thunderball*.

The 'rats in the sewer under Istanbul' scene was originally filmed using white laboratory rats coated in chocolate to make them look real. But the rats kept licking the chocolate off each other. Eventually they had to use real street rats.

Faithfulness to the novel 8/10.

Do say 'It is the best. Of all of them. Unquestionably. No argument.'
Also venture 'Actually, if they'd been looking for someone to play Bond as a convincing cold-blooded psychopath, they needn't have looked much further than Robert Shaw.'

DR NO
The Book (1958)
Bond is sent to Jamaica to investigate the death of Strangways (pronounced like that, not 'Strangeways'), the head of the Secret Service station there. Strangways' last investigation concerned Dr Julius No, owner of a private island called Crab Key. Bond teams up with Cayman Islander Quarrel (introduced in *Live and Let Die*), and steals out to the island. He meets Honeychile 'Honey' Rider (spelled 'Ryder' in the film), a gorgeous white Jamaican. All three are then chased by Dr No's men, and Quarrel is killed by a flame-throwing vehicle designed to look like a dragon.

What the critics seem to have found offensive about Bond is exactly what the rest of us love about him.

Bond and Honeychile are taken to Dr No's prison, built, inevitably, inside a mountain, where the criminal himself gives them dinner (or rather his servants do, as he has metal claws instead of hands). No tells them he's developed a device for sabotaging American missiles, with which he will hold the West to ransom. Bond, however, escapes and kills Dr No by dropping a huge bucket of animal dung on his head. Whatever comes to hand. ...

Memorable scene The novel begins with an account of Bond's survival after his poisoning in *From Russia with Love*. The culprit was tetrodotoxin, which is obtained from the reproductive organs of a pufferfish. If Bond were going to be poisoned by any part of a fish, it would have to be that part, wouldn't it?

Critics For the first time (to any great extent), Fleming was taken to task by the critics for salaciousness. The headline of a famous *New Statesman* review by Paul Johnson says it all: 'Sex, Snobbery and Sadism'. Don't waste your breath on a defence. Merely affect an expression of bemused surprise and utter the single word, 'Precisely.' What Johnson seems to have found offensive about Bond is exactly what the rest of us love about him.

MBV It's in this book that Bond starts using the Walther PPK 7.65mm. Until now, he has preferred a Beretta, but Fleming had received a letter from Bond fan Geoffrey Boothroyd, a gun enthusiast who thought the Beretta seemed more of a 'lady's gun', and said 007 needed something more powerful. Always amused to employ real names in his stories, Fleming christened the Secret Service armourer who persuades Bond to change his gun 'Major Boothroyd'.

The Film (1962)
The one where Ursula Andress wears the white bikini. That's really all you need to know. Oh, and the fact that it was the first ever Bond film.

Trivia Sean Connery has a phobia of spiders, so the scene where a tarantula crawls over him was filmed using a sheet of glass (look closely and you can see it). Suggest that this was reassuring for the tarantula, too, as it was rumoured to have a phobia of excessive chest hair.

> The one where Ursula Andress wears the white bikini. That's really all you need to know.

Fleming didn't think much of the film when he first saw it, and commented that he thought Cary Grant would have made a better Bond, though he changed his mind later.

Faithfulness to the novel 5/10.

Do say 'I think you'll find that in the novel Honeychile first appears as nature intended, apart from her knife belt.'
Don't say 'Wasn't *From Russia with Love* the first Bond film?' This is a common mistake made by those new to the Bond game.

GOLDFINGER
The Book (1959)
In this, the longest Fleming novel, Bond investigates Auric Goldfinger, England's richest man, suspected of smuggling gold out of the country. Bond exposes him as a card cheat (shades of *Moonraker*) and steals his girlfriend, Jill Masterton (changed to Masterson in the 1964 film). Goldfinger promptly suffocates Masterton by covering her in gold paint. Bond follows Goldfinger to Switzerland, realises he is a SMERSH agent, and discovers how he smuggles the gold: his Rolls-Royce is made of the stuff.

Bond and Tilly Masterton, seeking revenge for her sister's death, are captured by Goldfinger. He forces them to help in his robbery of Fort Knox. Bond foils the plan, kills Goldfinger and ends up with man-hating lesbian ally Pussy Galore. Not only has he turned her against Goldfinger, he's changed her mind about the 'lesbian' bit, too.

Memorable scene The golf game between Bond and Goldfinger at the 'Royal St Marks' club, a not-very-fictionalised version of Fleming's beloved Royal St George's Golf Club at Sandwich in Kent. A friend had told him of the trick by which the villain attempts to beat Bond: jumping up and down to flatten sand in the bunker, on the pretence that you can't see the hole.

By sad coincidence, it was after lunching at this golf club that Fleming suffered what he called 'the iron crab': a heart attack, which proved fatal the following morning. The food, it should be noted, was not to blame – not when you smoke 70 high-tar cigarettes a day.

Gold Auric Goldfinger's obsession with the world's most famous metal was an exaggerated version of Fleming's own. He collected gold coins, possessed (but didn't use) a gold typewriter, and even had a gold top made for his Bic biro. Gilding the lily is one thing, but gilding a disposable pen?

The film made famous the 'death by body paint' scene, with Shirley Eaton looking particularly memorable all in gold. Unfortunately, the notion that you can kill someone in this way is a myth.

MBV The villain's moniker came from Ernö Goldfinger, a modernist British architect. He was distinctly unimpressed with the use made of his name, even threatening legal action to halt the book's publication. Although this came to nothing, Fleming urged his publishers to change the surname to 'Goldprick' while it was still a possibility.

The Film (1964)
This is the one where Oddjob decapitates a statue with his hat after, arguably, the most famous golf match in cinema history. Most golfers' immediate reaction was to

wonder why the club secretary didn't march out and demand to know what the hell was going on. Answer: when Bond asks precisely that question, Goldfinger replies coldly that he owns the club. But that's not the most famous line in the film; that honour goes to the oft-quoted exchange between Goldfinger and Bond as the latter is about to be bisected (groin first) by a laser:

Bond 'Do you expect me to talk?'
Goldfinger 'No, Mr Bond. I expect you to die.'

Trivia Honor Blackman introduces herself to Bond with the line: 'My name is Pussy Galore.' The original script gave his reply as 'I know, but what's your name?' This was eventually changed to 'I must be dreaming.'

The movie featured Bond's most famous car, the silver Aston Martin DB5 with revolving number plates. Two were used in filming, with another two made for a promotional tour. One of these, bought for £5,000 in 1970, sold for $2,000,000 in 2006. SPECTRE always held the world to ransom; its agents could have made more money simply by stealing 007's car.

Faithfulness to the novel 6/10.

Do say 'Oddjob only has one line in the film: "Aha".' Hats off to you for knowing that.
Also say 'By far the best Bond film soundtrack, with the possible exception of "Diamonds Are Forever". It's no coincidence that they were both sung by Dame Shirley Bassey.'

ß

The producers reportedly considered asking Steven Spielberg, who was at the time in post-production with **Jaws**, *to direct* **The Spy Who Loved Me**. *But they decided to wait and see 'how the fish picture turns out'.*

THE SIXTIES

Marking a change of format by Fleming, who hitherto had written only full-length Bond novels, *For Your Eyes Only* (1960) is a collection of five short stories and, as such, a gift to the bluffer. You can be hazy on details, claiming for any one story that your recollections are lost among those of the other four. But you should, of course, show a familiarity with the broad outlines.

FROM A VIEW TO A KILL
The Short Story
Bond hides in a tree to shoot a Russian assassin who has been killing French dispatch riders carrying top secret documents from SHAPE (Supreme Headquarters Allied Powers Europe). That's about it.

The Film (1985)
This seventh and last outing for Roger Moore takes part of the title of the short story, and absolutely nothing else. Starting in Siberia and ending in San Francisco, there

isn't even a dispatch rider involved. Instead, there's a preposterous tale about a crazed megalomaniac intent on blowing up the San Andreas fault. And a scene involving someone parachuting off the Eiffel Tower.

Faithfulness to the story 0/10.

Do say 'Dear old Rog realised he should call it a day when he learned that, at the age of 57, he was older than his Bond girl's mother.'

FOR YOUR EYES ONLY
The Short Story
Bond avenges the death of two of M's friends, murdered by a former Gestapo officer to whom they refuse to sell their Jamaican home. He does this as a favour to M, so he's actually moonlighting on non-government business.

The Film (1981)
Probably best known for its risqué poster, where Roger Moore is framed between the open legs of a crossbow-wielding beauty in a swimsuit. It's also famous for the bobsled race.

Trivia Bernard Lee, who had played M since the first Bond movie, died while preparing for this film. Cubby Broccoli left the role vacant as a mark of respect.

One of the female characters is played by Cassandra Harris, the first wife of future Bond Pierce Brosnan.

Faithfulness to the story 3/10.

Don't say 'This is the only Bond film where a serving prime minister appears.' Almost true, but it was actress Janet Brown playing Margaret Thatcher.

RISICO
The Short Story
Bond breaks a drug-smuggling ring in Venice.

MBV The chase scene in Risico is set on the Lido beach, the same one that appears in *Death in Venice*. Make sure you mention this: the contrast between James Bond vigorously fighting drug smugglers and Dirk Bogarde with make-up running down his face is priceless.

The Film
There isn't one. Parts of the storyline were, however, used in the film *For Your Eyes Only*.

QUANTUM OF SOLACE
The Short Story
Bond hears about a woman's turbulent romantic history while attending a dinner in the governor's mansion in the Bahamas. Then he discovers that the rather dull woman he has been sitting next to is the person he has heard being described. The title is taken from the governor's explanation to Bond that when the 'Quantum of Solace' falls to zero, all consideration and compassion of one

human being for another is gone – and the relationship is finished. Not the usual Bond plot, then.

A reference to this story is particularly useful when faced with someone who sees Bond as all action, no depth. Here our hero realises that such tales make the 'violent dramatics' of his work seem 'hollow'.

The Film (2008)

This sequel to 2006's *Casino Royale* features Daniel Craig as Bond seeking revenge for the death of his lover Vesper Lynd. It bears no relation to the short story of the same name, and received 'mixed' reviews (a euphemism for 'mostly bad'). Of the film's title, Craig said it was 'meant to confuse a little – it's meant to make you sort of wonder'. Having seen the finished product, many fans wondered why they bothered.

Faithfulness to the story 0/10.

Do ask 'Why didn't they just call it *Casino Royale Part II*? It worked for *The Godfather*.'
Don't ask 'Does Dan get his testicles pulverised again?'

THE HILDEBRAND RARITY

The Short Story

Bond, on leave, discovers the body of Milton Krest, a loud-mouthed American millionaire touring the Seychelles in search of the unusual fish known as the Hildebrand Rarity. Krest had boasted of beating his wife Liz with 'the Corrector', a whip made from a ray's tail.

Cause of death? Someone had pushed the Hildebrand Rarity down his throat. And they say eating fish is good for you.

The Film
Again, there isn't one, although Milton Krest and 'the Corrector' were featured in the film *Licence to Kill*. So it seems unlikely that they'll appear again.

THUNDERBALL
The Book (1961)
Bond visits a health farm and achieves his aim of getting into shape despite a fellow guest (a gangster wishing to remain undiscovered) trying to kill him on the traction machine. Then the real action starts: SPECTRE, an international criminal organisation led by Ernst Stavro Blofeld (*see* 'Bond and Cricket', page 105), has stolen two atomic warheads from NATO, and is holding the world to ransom for £100 million (which was a lot of money in 1962).

Bond doesn't actually meet Blofeld in this novel; the enemy is SPECTRE's agent Emilio Largo, with his boat *Disco Volante* ('flying saucer' in Italian, Spanish and Portuguese, and the name of the third-best nightclub in Slough). Bond attacks the boat as it goes to retrieve the warheads. He has made Largo's girlfriend, Domino Vitali, aware that the villain had her brother killed. This pays off when Largo is about to kill Bond: Domino skewers him with a spear gun. Bond is rewarded with his life and the girl (*déjà vu* anyone?).

Memorable scene At the health farm, Bond exacts revenge for the traction-machine incident by locking Count Lippe (the gangster) into a sweatbox and turning the dial up to 180°F. This must be an entertaining mental image for anyone who has a personal trainer.

Lawsuits The story behind this story is very involved, but you can afford to keep it simple: Fleming and Kevin McClory cooperate on a film treatment, they fall out, lots of legal action. Fleming writes it as the novel, Connery stars in the film, McClory has the producer role on the film, agrees not to make another version of it for ten years. When the time's up, he gets Connery to return for his third stint as Bond in 1983's *Never Say Never Again*, essentially a remake of *Thunderball*. This was in the middle of Roger Moore's tour of duty. And they say spy novels are complicated. ...

MBV The book's title is taken from the phrase coined by US soldiers to describe the mushroom cloud resulting from an atomic bomb.

The Film (1965)
The one where Bond escapes over a wall using a jetpack on his back. It also has a memorable underwater fight scene at the end.

Trivia Connery's problems with animals continue: the plastic screens protecting him from sharks weren't high enough and some of his reaction shots show real terror as the predators get too close for comfort. As an aside, Tom Jones fainted as he sang the title song's final high note.

Faithfulness to the novel 6/10.

Do ask 'Haven't I seen that Count Lippe before?' Answer: you probably have. He was played by New Zealand actor Guy Doleman, who was Harry Palmer's memorably suave boss in *The Ipcress File*.

THE SPY WHO LOVED ME
The Book (1962)

The novel marked a significant break with Bond tradition. It is told in the first person by the central female character, Vivienne Michel, and Bond doesn't appear until two-thirds of the way through.

Michel, a Canadian, relates her experiences of being treated badly by men while working on a newspaper in London. She ends up in New York State, where she gets a job at a motel. Two thugs called Sluggsy and Horror (Seriously? Did Fleming use these names for a bet?), who have come to burn the place down, sexually assault her.

Bond just happens to arrive looking for a room (these things happen in novels), and during a prolonged fight sequence kills the thugs. He beds Michel, but has gone by morning, having captured her heart. This is the closest Fleming gets to writing serious erotic fiction.

The local police chief warns her of the dangers of falling for dangerous men, saying that Bond is no better than the thugs. As if being told that something is bad for you ever stopped anyone.

Memorable scene In a flashback, Vivienne nearly loses her virginity to a schoolboy in a private box at the back of a cinema, but the manager bursts in and stops them. The scene was based on Fleming's own first sexual experience in the Royalty Kinema, Windsor. Except that there was no manager, and thus no 'nearly'.

Backlash The novel was slated by critics and public alike. A good reader's quote to use is: 'Now look here, Fleming, this catering to fifth-form eroticism must stop. Do you hear?' Fleming claimed he had written the book to stop children seeing Bond as a hero. But, admitting that the plan had gone 'very much awry', he asked his publishers if they would agree not to reprint the book or issue a paperback. The success of the Bond films (the first one, *Dr No*, appeared the same year) meant the answer was ... well, one of the words in that film title.

MBV To add credibility to the story, Fleming gave Vivienne Michel a 'co-author' credit on the book's title page.

The Film (1977)
The one where Bond skis off the mountain only to deploy a Union Jack parachute. The breath-stopping silence before the parachute opens tends to live on in the memory of everyone who's seen it.

This is Roger Moore's favourite Bond film.

Trivia The metal teeth worn by Richard Kiel to play Jaws (who reappeared in the next Bond film) were so painful that he could only keep them in for a few seconds at a time. His stuntman recreated the effect using orange peel wrapped in aluminium foil.

The producers reportedly considered asking Steven Spielberg, who was at the time in post-production with *Jaws*, to direct the film. But they decided to wait and see 'how the fish picture turns out'. Why Spielberg? There is a shark scene in the film and they assumed he was something of an expert in this department. This is how producers' minds work.

Faithfulness to the novel 0/10.

Do ask 'Isn't that Bond girl Barbara Bach married to Ringo Starr? What did she see in the multimillionaire former Beatle?'

ON HER MAJESTY'S SECRET SERVICE
The Book (1963)
Bond, who at the start of the novel is tired of the Secret Service and wants to resign, is offered a million pounds by a Corsican gangland boss to marry his beautiful but highly strung daughter, Teresa 'Tracy' di Vicenzo, after Bond has saved her from committing suicide by drowning. Only Bond could refuse an offer like this, but he does agree to stay with Tracy (he has already slept with her once) if the boss, Draco, tells him where Blofeld can be found – Bond has spent the time since *Thunderball* hunting him.

Bond investigates Blofeld's Swiss mountain hideaway, but when his cover is blown he gets chased by the criminal's henchmen. Tracy helps to rescue him, and he proposes marriage. You see, Bond will marry for love but not for money – he's a romantic after all. Tracy accepts. Back in England, Bond discovers that Blofeld is planning biological warfare against Britain, using ten beautiful girls as unwitting virus-carriers. Bond returns to blow up the hideaway, but Blofeld escapes. Bond and Tracy marry on New Year's Day, but as they drive off, Blofeld appears, overtakes and shoots at them; sadly, Tracy is killed.

Memorable scene It can only be the final four paragraphs, where Bond cradles his dead wife, telling the policeman who's arrived at the accident, 'She's having a rest', then whispering into her hair, 'We have all the time in the world.'

Errors Fleming, who prided himself on the accuracy of his research, was annoyed to learn that he had made several mistakes in the book. One of the errors was about one of the really important things in life; no, not guns or bombs or cars – champagne. Fleming had mentioned a half-bottle of Pol Roger. Pol Roger didn't make half-bottles.

MBV This, the first novel to be published after the start of the Bond films, contains two in-jokes. Fleming, initially sceptical about Sean Connery, was sufficiently impressed to include a reference from Bond to his

Scottish father. And when Bond eats at the Piz Gloria restaurant, he spots Ursula Andress at a nearby table.

The Film (1969)

Australian actor George Lazenby makes his first and only appearance as James Bond. Allegedly he got the job by inventing a curriculum vitae and playing the strong silent type when he first met the film's producers. Before the cameras started to roll, Lazenby confessed all to the film's director, Peter Hunt. In an article in the *New York Post*, he was quoted as follows. 'I said "Peter, I've never acted a day in my life. I've modeled but never spoken in front of a camera." And he's looking at me, "What? And you say you can't act? You've fooled two of the most ruthless men I've ever met in my life. Stick to your story, and I'll make you the next James Bond."' This is probably the biggest bluff in the history of Bond.

Trivia Diana Rigg reportedly disliked Lazenby so much that she deliberately ate garlic before filming love scenes with him. Both actors have since claimed that this is an urban myth.

OHMSS demonstrates an early example of the Bond movies' in-jokes: in one scene, a cleaner can be heard whistling the theme tune from *Goldfinger*.

Faithfulness to the novel 6/10.

Don't say 'I think Lazenby was much underrated as Bond. He showed real depth in the Fry's Chocolate Cream advert.'

Do say 'In the film it's Irma Bunt who kills Tracy. Blofeld is driving in his neck brace.'

YOU ONLY LIVE TWICE
The Book (1964)

Bond's work is suffering terribly after the murder of his wife. M revokes his licence to kill, changing him from 007 to 7777. He is sent to Japan to persuade Tiger Tanaka, head of the country's intelligence service, to share information about the Soviets. Tiger agrees, provided Bond can kill Dr Shatterhand, a mysterious Westerner who is inducing Japanese people to commit suicide.

Aided by Kissy Suzuki (whose name is never mentioned in the film), a beautiful Japanese girl, Bond goes to the castle owned by Shatterhand, who is none other than his wife's killer, Blofeld. Bond is captured, but manages to strangle Blofeld. In escaping, he sustains a head injury that wipes his memory, and for nearly a year lives with Kissy as a fisherman on a remote island. But then he sees the word 'Vladivostok' in a newspaper; it evokes faint memories that he once fought the country in which that city lies. Kissy knows he must return to his former life, so reluctantly lets him go. There are several ways of ending a relationship with just one word, but 'Vladivostok' must be a first.

Memorable scene Tiger Tanaka explains to Bond how martial-arts fighters can withstand seemingly incapacitating blows to the groin: they've been trained to withdraw their testicles back into their bodies (a technique only Samurai warriors are said to have the ability to do). Given Le Chiffre's use of the carpet beater in *Casino Royale,* Bond might be forgiven for wishing he'd mastered this skill himself.

More ennui In *Thunderball,* Bond's health is waning; in *The Spy Who Loved Me* he's absent for over half the book; in *On Her Majesty's Secret Service* he wants to resign; at the start of this novel he's depressed and error-prone, and at the end he has even forgotten who he is. The reality is that Bond's slide into oblivion, only to be rescued each time and brought back for another book, matched that of his creator.

Fleming, increasingly unwell, was growing bored with 007 (again), and toyed constantly with his destruction. The Bond films had made him more money than he ever could have dreamed of, and yet, when a friend asked him what success meant, he replied: 'Ashes, old boy. Just ashes.'

MBV Here, you're spoilt for choice. First, while researching the novel in Japan, Fleming ate raw lobster and drank turtle blood. Second, Kissy becomes pregnant with Bond's child, but chooses never to reveal this to him.

The title of the book comes from a poem written by Fleming in the style of the Japanese poet Basho (1643–94): 'You only live twice/Once when you are born/And once when you look death in the face.'

The Film (1967)
This was the first Bond film to diverge radically from the plot of the original novel. This might have been because

the screenplay was written by Roald Dahl, who doubtless wanted to put his own mark on the project. Suffice it to say that Fleming would not have been impressed. He'd died three years earlier, though he might well have succeeded in cursing the production from beyond the grave (*see* below).

Trivia Blofeld, played by Donald Pleasence in this, the first film in which the character's face was revealed, had his trademark white cat. Unfortunately, the animal was so traumatised by explosions in the final scene that it scarpered and was only found several days later, hiding in the set.

While filming from a helicopter, crew member Johnny Jordan's foot was almost severed by the rotors of another helicopter blown out of control by a wind gust. His foot had to be amputated, but Jordan worked on the next Bond film wearing an artificial one. Even 007's cameramen are fearless.

The producers diced with death too. Due to return from a location-scouting trip, Broccoli and Saltzman, along with three members of the production team, attended a last-minute meeting and subsequently missed their flight (number 911) out of Tokyo. The plane disintegrated over Mount Fuji, killing everyone on board.

MBV This was the only Bond film to be filmed almost entirely in one country. Japan was one of the few things the film had in common with the book. Furthermore, this is the first Bond film in which 007 doesn't visit Britain at all.

Faithfulness to the novel 2/10.

Don't say 'The similarities between scar-faced, Nehru-suit-wearing, cat-stroking Dr Evil in *Austin Powers* and Donald Pleasence's portrayal of Blofeld are purely coincidental.'

THE MAN WITH THE GOLDEN GUN
The Book (1965)

This was Ian Fleming's final Bond novel, written when ill health had reduced his capacity for work. Sadly, it shows. Bond returns from Vladivostok where the Russians have brainwashed him to kill M. He fails, and after rehabilitation is sent to his old haunt, Jamaica, to put an end to the antics of Francisco 'Pistols' Scaramanga, whose gold-plated Colt .45 has dispatched several Secret Service operatives. Bond infiltrates Scaramanga's gang, learning of plans to torch sugar-cane fields so that Fidel Castro can control the world market. Bond is wounded by one of Scaramanga's poisoned bullets, but kills the villain. He recuperates in the arms of Jamaican Secret Service station agent, Mary Goodnight (at least she's not called 'Goodhead' this time).

Memorable scene Sadly, you'd be conning people if you claimed that any of the scenes in this book are memorable. And conning is against the bluffer's code.

Farewell The book was published after Fleming's death. There are rumours that it was edited by novelist and

Bond fan Kingsley Amis, but the consensus seems to be that Amis only offered advice. One of his unheeded suggestions was that Scaramanga be sexually attracted to Bond. As if the villain's third nipple wasn't enough for shocked readers to cope with.

MBV This is the only novel in which M's name (Vice Admiral Sir Miles Messervy) is mentioned; until this point it had been 'censored' by dashes.

The Film (1974)
Universally panned by the critics, this was one of the lowest-grossing films of the Bond genre. Roger Moore's eyebrows were up and down like a fiddler's elbow, and it was generally thought that it was being played too much for laughs. On the other hand, Christopher Lee, who played the excessively nippled Scaramanga, was generally thought to be one of the best Bond villains of all time.

Trivia Christopher Lee was a distant step-cousin of Fleming, who wanted him to play Dr No in the first Bond film.

Also of considerable interest to the bluffer is that this was the first Bond movie ever to be shown in the Kremlin.

Faithfulness to the novel 2/10.

Do say 'Did you know that Alice Cooper wrote a song called "The Man with the Golden Gun" that was originally meant to be the theme tune? They chose Lulu's version instead.'

Also say 'Alice's version appears on his hit album *Muscle of Love*. Even Scaramanga preferred it to Lulu's.'

OCTOPUSSY
The Short Story
Bond confronts a retired British army major living in (where else?) Jamaica, forcing him to admit to a wartime murder. 007 allows him time to reflect; the major takes the simple way out, committing suicide by forcing a poisonous fish (what is this obsession with fish?) to attack him.

The Film (1983)
The one with the killer yo-yos and Steven Berkoff 'chewing the scenery' (overacting) as the baddie. It had a rather good promotional poster with an eight-armed Maud Adams (Octopussy) behind a gun-toting Roger Moore. Besides the name, it has nothing in common with the short story.

Trivia This was the last Bond movie to announce its successor in the closing credits.

Look out for the cyclist who swerves between two vehicles during the car chase scene in India. He's not a stuntman, just a local who happened to ride on to the set.

Faithfulness to the story 0/10.

Do ask 'Why was she called "Octopussy"?'
Don't ask 'What is it with Fleming and the word "pussy"?'

THE PROPERTY OF A LADY

The Short Story

Bond unearths the KGB's head man in London by spotting him at an auction, where he is bidding for a Fabergé egg as cover for paying a double agent. Fleming originally wrote the story for Sotheby's auction house for inclusion in its yearbook, *The Ivory Hammer*. He was so dissatisfied with his effort that he refused to take a fee – something he clearly had not learned to do in his early career as a stockbroker.

The Film

There isn't one, although part of the story was used as a scene in *Octopussy* (the film).

THE LIVING DAYLIGHTS

The Short Story

Bond is sent to Berlin to kill a Russian assassin who is due to shoot a British agent. The assassin turns out to be a beautiful blonde cellist, and Bond makes a spontaneous decision to shoot her rifle butt rather than her. Everybody survives, but Bond considers the mission to be a failure.

The Film (1987)

Timothy Dalton makes his brooding, troubled, humourless, somewhat underrated debut, and uses a cello case belonging to Bond girl Kara Milovy (played by Maryam d'Abo) as an unusual means of escape. The very beginning of the film is faithful to the original story, but then it veers off into predictable Bond super-villain territory.

Trivia John Barry, who was providing the score for his last Bond film, also took a cameo role in the final scene, as Kara's orchestra leader.

Faithfulness to the story 3/10.

Do say 'Timothy Dalton proved to be a very accomplished light comic actor in the 2007 comedy *Hot Fuzz*.'

—— *ß* ——

Bond was never likely to die with his creator. He was far too valuable a literary and cinematic property for that. So it is hardly surprising that there is a long succession of leading contemporary novelists who willingly stepped into Ian Fleming's shoes.

THE POST-FLEMING ERA

THE WRITERS

In any consideration of Fleming's legacy, you must take a firm standpoint on the literary merit of the Bond books he wrote in the decade or so before he died.

Your summarising remarks about the Fleming/Bond books should focus on the serious side, such as:

* The depth of 007's character.
* His reflections on the nature of evil (as in *Casino Royale*).
* His ability to appreciate wider life rather than the narrow field of his work (as in *Quantum of Solace*).

If, however, you find yourself in the company of people who persist in seeing Bond as childish, deflect them, not by arguing but by agreeing with them. Taking the wind from your opponents' sails is far more effective than stoking up a fight. And you don't need to look any further than Fleming himself for ammunition. Talking about Bond, he said: 'He's what you would expect of an adolescent mind – which I happen to possess.'

But Bond was never likely to die with his creator. He was far too valuable a literary and cinematic property for that. So it is hardly surprising that there is a long succession of leading contemporary novelists who willingly stepped into Ian Fleming's shoes. Here is a rundown of the main pretenders.

Kingsley Amis (1968)

Amis, one of the finest comic novelists of his generation, was best known for his debut novel *Lucky Jim* in 1954. A great admirer of the Bond novels, he unhesitatingly took on the task of continuing the series, albeit under the pseudonym Robert Markham. His first and only Bond novel was *Colonel Sun* (1968).

Plot M is kidnapped by Colonel Sun of the Chinese People's Liberation Army (perhaps a new form of Chinese takeaway). Bond has to rescue his boss from a Greek island, which of course he does, in the process gaining the gratitude of the Soviet Union, which offers 007 a medal. He declines.

Trivia Fleming's widow, Ann, wasn't overly chuffed about the decision to hire Kingsley Amis to write this book, dismissing him as a 'left-wing opportunist'.

MBV Amis continued Fleming's cheeky habit of including real people in the novel. He used the names of friends, as well as those he had met during his research in Greece. Even the name of a boat Bond uses (*The Altair*) was taken from reality: it was the boat Amis and his wife used on holiday.

John Gardner (1981–96)

The British thriller writer carried the 007 torch for nearly two decades, producing 14 novels (plus two novelisations of Bond films). He rooted Bond in the real world – for instance, the 1989 book *Win, Lose or Die* features a plot by the Brotherhood of Anarchy and Secret Terrorism (what a 1970s punk band that might have been …) to infiltrate and blow up the Royal Navy vessel hosting a summit between George Bush Sr, Margaret Thatcher and Mikhail Gorbachev. Bond, needless to say, saves the day.

Gardner may have been a Brit, but because these novels were published by the American firm G.P. Putnam's Sons, the deathly hand of Uncle Sam began to reach across the prose. For instance, in 1991's *The Man from Barbarossa*, a waiter wears 'pants' rather than trousers. If Ann Fleming objected to left-wing opportunists, God knows what she would have thought of that. Just as well she died in 1981, then.

Raymond Benson (1996–2002)

The Americanisation of the Bond writing process was completed in 1996, when duties were handed over to US author Raymond Benson. In the next six years he produced six novels, three short stories and three novelisations of 007 films. He may have been a Yank, but it wasn't all bad news for Bond traditionalists; Benson made the decision to give the spy his old gun, the Walther PPK, back. It had been previously removed by Gardner.

One of the short stories was 1999's *Midsummer Night's Doom,* in which Bond attends a party at the Playboy Mansion in Beverly Hills. Understandable: the story was for *Playboy* magazine. But Bond isn't there for the reasons you might assume (and indeed, he might have hoped for); he has to prevent some Ministry of Defence secrets from being sold to the Russian Mafia. Why this transaction should have taken place *chez* Hugh Hefner isn't entirely clear, but that's the world of Bond for you.

Finally, in referring to the Benson years you should have this irresistible point of information at your fingertips: in his 1997 story *Blast from the Past,* the writer introduces James Suzuki, Bond's only child, to his father for the first time. Unfortunately he is murdered shortly afterwards, thus depriving future producers of the opportunity of capitalising on a whole new raft of storylines. (On the other hand, the 'death' could all have been a cunning ruse to keep Bond Jr out of the firing line, and in fact he's out there somewhere, waiting to make his first big screen entrance. Just think of the commercial opportunities in Japan!)

Sebastian Faulks (2008)

After Benson hung up his typewriter, the Fleming estate turned to highbrow British novelist Sebastian Faulks (of *Birdsong* fame). His Bond novel, *Devil May Care*, was published on 28 May 2008, to coincide with what would have been Ian Fleming's 100th birthday. Faulks not only returned our hero to his original era of the 1960s (Gardner and Benson had both updated him to the modern world), he also copied the original author's methods of working. 'In his house in Jamaica,' explained Faulks, 'Ian Fleming used to write a thousand words in the morning, then go snorkelling, have a cocktail, lunch on the terrace, more diving, another thousand words in the late afternoon, then more martinis and glamorous women. In my house in London, I followed this routine exactly – apart from the cocktails, the lunch and the snorkelling.'

Faulks's contract allowed him the option of writing a second novel, but he declined to take this up. 'Once funny, twice silly, three times a slap, as the nanny saying goes,' he explained.

Jeffery Deaver (2011)

Back over the pond again, this time to American thriller expert Jeffery Deaver. Perhaps the most notable thing about his book, *Carte Blanche* (set in the modern day), was that Bond doesn't smoke. There are liberties you can take and liberties you can't – and you must insist that this one simply can't be taken.

William Boyd (2013)

And just to carry on the pattern, the next Bond author is a Brit. Like Faulks, Boyd decided to set his story *Solo* in the 1960s. With time-travel habits like this, James Bond is fast becoming the new Doctor Who.

Anthony Horowitz (2015–18)

The author of the Alex Rider novels, documenting the adventures of a teenage spy, seemed a natural fit for the Bond series. And so it proved, with first *Trigger Mortis* and then *Forever and a Day* receiving widespread critical praise. As part of a charity auction, Horowitz offered bidders the chance to appear in *Forever and a Day*. The winning bid came from Reade Griffith, who featured as a CIA agent. But Joann McPike's bid was so generous that she also got to grace the book's pages. Horowitz included her as Joanne Brochet. The surname is French for 'pike' (linguistic cunning of a type that Fleming would have appreciated).

Charlie Higson (2005–)
Bluffers should also know that Charlie Higson, of *The Fast Show* fame, documented the adventures of the schoolboy Bond in five novels and one short story. This series has since been taken over by Steve Cole.

THE FILMS
Now it's time to get on to the films that owe nothing to anything that was written by Ian Fleming other than the character of James Bond. Still, in order to be a top bluffer, you'll need to know something about them.

LICENCE TO KILL (1989)
This is the film where Bond's CIA pal, Felix Leiter, loses a leg to a shark. 'He disagreed with something that ate him', remarks Timothy Dalton's Bond in a rare excursion into wry humour.

Trivia Due to cigarette product placement, the United States Surgeon General insisted on a 'dangers of smoking' warning in the closing credits. There's also a scene where a burning man falls into a lorry full of petrol, but no one seemed too bothered about that.

The scene where Bond resigns from MI6 was shot at Ernest Hemingway's house in Key West, Florida. When M tells him that his licence to kill is to be revoked, Bond responds: 'I guess this is a farewell to arms'. an allusion to Hemingway's famous novel of the same name. Dalton wasn't allowed much more in the way of one-liners, so he must have been grateful for these opportunities (*see* page XX for a selection of Bond's best one-liners).

During the scene where 007 is hanging by a hook over the cocaine grinder, Benicio Del Toro's character has to cut him loose. While filming, he actually cut Dalton's hand, and the scene had to be stopped so Dalton could be stitched up.

GOLDENEYE (1995)

The one with Xenia Onatopp, the woman who can kill a man by crushing him between her legs during the act of lovemaking. This film was the first of Pierce Brosnan's four outings as Her Majesty's best-known spy.

Trivia In the scene where Bond chases a villain through the streets of St Petersburg in a tank, the tank crashes through a truck carrying cans of Perrier water. Nice bit of product placement for Perrier, but after filming they collected every last can from the set, crushed or not, to stop rivals from stealing them and selling other water in them.

Before filming had even begun, Brosnan hurt his hand at home in Malibu. In several scenes a hand double was used – none other than Brosnan's adopted son, Christopher, whose uncle was hellraising Irish actor Richard Harris.

TOMORROW NEVER DIES (1997)

Another Brosnan-as-Bond, but here Jonathan Pryce stars as a crazed media magnate. All characters appearing in this work are fictitious. Any resemblance to Rupert Murdoch is purely coincidental.

Trivia A scene in a car park had to be reshot, but budget considerations meant that instead of going back to Germany, where the original scene had been filmed, the producers used Brent Cross shopping centre in north London. Some 17 BMWs were used, and posters had to be put up for the ten days of filming advising shoppers that the explosions were nothing to worry about.

In another scene, Bond and his ally, Wai Lin, played by Michelle Yeoh, argue about who should drive a motorbike they're both about to get on. The director achieved his desired level of realism by only introducing this element of arguing just before shooting the scene. He took Brosnan and Yeoh aside separately, neither knowing the other had been spoken to, and told each of them not to let the other get into the driver's seat.

THE WORLD IS NOT ENOUGH (1999)

In this one, Robert Carlyle, of *Trainspotting* fame, plays the villain who can't feel any pain because his brain has a bullet lodged in it.

Trivia One of the scenes involved shooting near the real-life headquarters of Bond's employer, MI6, next to Vauxhall Bridge in London. When this became known, MI6 banned it, saying such filming would amount to a security risk. A campaign was started to overturn the decision, and eventually Foreign Secretary Robin Cook ordered that filming should be allowed to take place. 'After all Bond has done for Britain,' he said, 'it was the least we could do for Bond.'

The warehouse owned by Valentin Zukovsky, played for laughs by Robbie Coltrane, has posters of scantily clad women on its walls. These are all former Bond girls.

DIE ANOTHER DAY (2002)

The one with Halle Berry as the Bond girl, and John Cleese taking over from Desmond Llewelyn as Q.

Trivia There were rumours that Cleese's character was going to be called 'R'. Pierce Brosnan expressed his relief that these rumours proved to be unfounded, because he said his Irish accent made it difficult for him to pronounce that letter.

In one scene Bond is shown unlocking a secret door at the south end of Westminster Bridge and descending to a disused Tube station, the fictional 'Vauxhall Cross', which MI6 now uses as a storeroom and testing facility for new equipment. A Tube map on the wall shows this station to have been on the Piccadilly Line, yet in reality the Piccadilly Line goes nowhere near here, and certainly never goes south of the River Thames.

At one point, MI6 double agent Miranda Frost, played by Rosamund Pike, says: 'I know all about you, 007. Sex for dinner, death for breakfast.' The last three words are the title of chapter 11 of the book version of *On Her Majesty's Secret Service*.

In one scene, Bond picks up a book called *A Field Guide to Birds of the West Indies*. You'll remember that this was a real book, written by one James Bond, and was where Ian Fleming got the name of his hero.

Also up there in terms of essential bluffing knowledge is the identity of Bond villain Toby Stephen's real life mother and father (*see* Glossary). If you didn't know that already, you really do need this book. Even more so if you didn't know that Madonna made an uncredited appearance as Verity (a fencing instructor) probably taking time out from contributing one of the most forgettable Bond theme songs.

SKYFALL (2012)

This is the one where Bond finally gets to be directed by someone who's won an Oscar (Sam Mendes for *American Beauty*). The villain is played by Javier Bardem, a jowly Spaniard who specialises in playing sociopaths (e.g., the assassin in the Coen Brothers' *No Country for Old Men*). The Bond girl is a little-known, smouldering, dark-eyed French stunner called Bérénice Marlohe (or Bernie Marlowe in English). The biggest shock of the film comes right at the end, as Judi Dench's M, injured in the gun battle with Javier Bardem, succumbs to her wounds and dies. It's a sign of the national affection in which both the character and Dench herself are held that the twist remained a secret. An unspoken agreement seemed to be heeded that no one would mention it to friends who were yet to see the film. Even those visiting the cinema weeks after the movie's release were none the wiser. You could say this is the ultimate tribute to the Bond franchise – the spy has taught us all how to keep our mouths shut when we have to.

Trivia Bond reaches his half-century in this movie, or at least his on-screen persona does, the film (the 23rd in the series) being released 50 years after the premiere of *Dr No*. That would make Bond a killing machine of about 88 in real terms.

Ben Whishaw, the somewhat effete Daniel Day-Lewis lookalike, takes the role of Q, meaning that for the first time, the character is younger than Bond. For those who grew up in the Desmond Llewelyn era this is somewhat akin to the world spinning into deep space.* And just when we'd got used to Basil Fawlty in the role.

You might also mention that a pub near one of the movie's filming locations in Scotland attempted to cash in on the connection with a series of hilariously unfunny Bond-themed meals. These included 'For Your Pies Only', 'Her Majesty's Secret Sandwich' and 'Scaramanga Scampi'.

Far funnier was the joke about the (fictional) pub landlord telling a friend that he 'had that Bond villain in last week – he was being rude to everyone and getting into fights'. 'Javier Bardem?' asks the friend. 'No,' replies the landlord, 'I've said he can come back if he behaves himself.'

SPECTRE (2015)

The one where Blofeld appears in an official Bond film for the first time since 1981's *For Your Eyes Only*. And even then he was unnamed, due to ongoing legal battles with Kevin McClory (*see* 'Thunderball: Lawsuits', page 64). If you want the last 'proper' appearance of Blofeld, it was in *Diamonds Are Forever*, as portrayed by Charles Gray.

Trivia The first Bond soundtrack not to be graced by the trumpet playing of Derek Watkins. He had performed on every film since *Dr No*, but sadly died after the release of *Skyfall*. Such a mundane name might initially appear out of keeping with the glamour of 007 – but you can remind your audience that Ian Fleming deliberately christened his character 'James Bond' because he wanted a plain, dull name. As such Derek Watkins was a perfect fit.

During production, nine customised luxury Land Rovers and Range Rovers, valued at $1 million, intended for filming in the Austrian Alps, were stolen from a car park in Germany. Rather an embarrassing lack of security on a movie about the world's most successful Secret Service agent.

NO TIME TO DIE (2020)

At the time of writing the 25th film in the series was still in production. It has attracted particular attention for the recruitment of award winning *Killing Eve* and *Fleabag* star Phoebe Waller-Bridge as one of the screenwriters. Quite why EON got the idea that a Bond movie needed the help of someone whose previous work featured complicated sexual relationships and excessive consumption of alcohol is anyone's guess.

UNOFFICIAL FILMS

There have been two non-EON Bond films due to complex rights issues, which you needn't try to figure out. You would be in good company since it would seem that, very often, the parties involved haven't entirely figured them out either. We therefore recommend a swift and uncompromising rejection of both. One is the original version of *Casino Royale (see* page 41).

The other, released in 1983, is *Never Say Never Again*. Essentially a remake of *Thunderball*, this one pitted Sean Connery, in his second comeback, against Roger Moore in *Octopussy*. Connery *really* should have said 'Never again', especially with that hairpiece.

But both these films, despite being unofficial, are well known. For maximum bluffing points you need to regale your audience with the charming and unlikely tale of *The Second Shot Kills*. This was a 1972 Bond movie which, although not made by EON, actually had the blessing of Cubby Broccoli. The film was the idea of 15-year-old Welsh schoolboys Keith Stephens-Borg and David Harnett. They had just spent 11 months and £50 making a version of the Arthur Conan-Doyle novel *The Lost World*, in which they used a local park in their native Newport as the Amazon basin where the dinosaurs still roam. Inspired by the experience, the budding film-makers turned their attention to 007. They wrote a script. Not wishing to get into trouble over copyright, they then contacted Broccoli. Crammed into a red telephone box with friends, they got through to the great man's secretary. 'We could hear him in the background saying we couldn't make the film,' recalls Stephens-Borg. 'He then asked if it was a home video, and we said yes, then he said good luck with it. We took that to mean he had given his permission.' With *cojones* like that the pair could probably have made it into the real Secret Service, never mind made films about the fictional one.

Stephens-Borg himself played Bond, with Harnett directing. Shooting took place around Newport, in the city's docks and atop its Transporter Bridge. The budget was £200, the equipment was wind-up cameras and 8mm film. At one point a replica gun got the boys into trouble – a cast member showed it off in a pub ('not a good idea,' admits Harnett), with the result that filming was halted, the gun was confiscated and the cast member spent a night in the police cells.

Fast forward nearly half a century and the friends decided to dig out their masterpiece, digitally restore it and even shoot some extra scenes. They bought vintage cameras and old film stock, while Keith's daughter Dawn appeared as their leading lady. Woolacombe beach in Devon doubled as Rio de Janeiro (clearly time hadn't dimmed the pair's imagination), and Keith made a camera dolly from PVC pipes and the wheels off a skateboard. A professional touch was added by the veteran actor Joss Ackland, who happened to be a neighbour of Keith and liked the sound of the project. He agreed to provide the voice of M. The finished result was screened in Cardiff in 2019. Not since the glory days of Timothy Dalton had Wales had such a strong connection with 007.

* See *The Bluffer's Guide to the Quantum Universe* for elucidation.

OH, JAMES ...

Given the way that 'Bond girl' has slipped into the national lexicon, it's only fair to examine the role of women in Bond's world. Studying the man without studying his women would be a bit like eating strawberries without cream.

His ideal companion is described by our hero in *Diamonds Are Forever* (the novel): 'Gold hair. Grey eyes. A sinful mouth. Perfect figure.' So far, so Peter Stringfellow. But then Mr Bond gets a little more sophisticated. 'And of course, she's got to be witty and poised and know how to dress and play cards and so forth. The usual things.'

The trouble is, being witty and playing cards is about as far as he wants it to go. 'Women were for recreation,' goes Bond's thinking in *Casino Royale*. 'On a job, they got in the way and fogged things up with sex and hurt feelings and all the emotional baggage they carried around. One had to look out for them and take care of them.' In this line of thinking he was only echoing his boss, M, who in *From Russia with Love* advises 007 to steer clear of those with two X chromosomes: 'Doesn't do to get mixed up with neurotic women in this business. They hang on to your gun arm, if you know what I mean.'

This jaundiced view of women – or at least of relationships with them – was, like so much else in Bond's world, a mirror of the life of Ian Fleming himself. He always ended flings by giving the girl a copy of *Toi et Moi*, a set of French poems about an affair that ends with the man and woman arguing on the doorstep of his flat as the rain pelts down. They say goodbye, but she doesn't have an umbrella, so comes back into the flat to wait for the weather to improve. The two of them sit there, disillusioned and unhappy. Talk about giving someone a hint.

Although Bond is famous for the extent of his sexual shenanigans, in the novels he rarely practises infidelity. A counter-intuitive fact to slip into conversation (people like counter-intuition – it's almost as good as counter-espionage) is that there are only two books, *Goldfinger* and *Thunderball*, where 007 sleeps with more than one woman. You could call him the original serial monogamist.

Some people have put forward the theory that the inspiration for all the Bond girls was a woman called Muriel Wright. She was a woman Ian Fleming met in 1935, when she was 26. 'Exceptionally beautiful', she was a talented horse-rider, polo player and skier, independently wealthy and a model. Not surprisingly, Fleming took a shine to her, a shine that she reflected straight back at him. Madly in love with him, she stayed devoted even though he did what 007 doesn't do: namely played the field (aren't the euphemisms men come up with for infidelity wonderful?). Tragedy struck in 1944, when Wright was killed in an air raid. Fleming was devastated, and called her 'too good to be true'. Could it be, then, that she made her way into his fiction?

Either way, you should be armed with her story. And you should also memorise the following facts about Bond's on-screen partners. Bond loves his women – and we all love a bit of trivia about his women.

URSULA ANDRESS

In *Dr No,* she looked great as Honey Ryder, emerging from the sea in her white bikini, but looking great was the limit of her contribution. Her Swiss accent was so strong that every line she delivers was dubbed by an actress called Nikki van der Zyl, who in true Bond style has an alias; she's often referred to as 'Monica'.

She looked great as Honey Ryder, emerging from the sea in her white bikini – but looking great was the limit of her contribution.

Despite the fact that she herself was German, van der Zyl's impeccable voice skills got her the job of revoicing not just Andress but every other female character in the film other than Miss Moneypenny and a Chinese girl. Not content with that (and despite the fact that her fee was a paltry £150), van der Zyl went on to overdub various female voices in every Bond film up to *The Man with the Golden Gun,* including Shirley Eaton in *Goldfinger* and some of Jane Seymour's lines in *Live and Let Die*. She even worked as dialogue coach to Gert Fröbe, who played the eponymous villain in *Goldfinger*. The German actor's English was so limited that he learned some of his lines phonetically, delivering them without knowing their meaning.

Finally – and this really proves the woman's mettle – Nikki van der Zyl overdubbed Raquel Welch's grunting in *One Million Years BC*. Be careful how you deploy this information, though; there are some men who might go all glassy-eyed at the mere thought of it.

Your real killer fact about Ursula Andress herself, meanwhile, is that she was once the girlfriend of James Dean. Their relationship was turbulent; at one point it was reported that Dean was learning German so that the two could 'argue in another language'.

Were it not for a chance decision, we might have been denied that legendary sight of the white-bikini-clad Ursula walking out of the waves: on the day James Dean fatally crashed his Porsche, he'd asked Andress to go with him, but she declined the offer.

EUNICE GAYSON

Eunice Gayson played Sylvia Trench in the first two Bond films, *Dr No* and *From Russia with Love*. Trench was going to be a recurring character in all the films, but the producers, in a very Bond-like moment, got bored and dropped her.

The Gayson genes live on in the 007 canon, though; her daughter Kate was an extra in 1995's *GoldenEye*. And Eunice will always be sure of a place in every Bond fan's heart; it is she who sets up perhaps the most famous line in any of the films. Seated at a casino table in *Dr No*, she says, 'I admire your luck, Mr…?' To which Sean Connery replies: 'Bond, James Bond.' Indeed were it not for Gayson the line might never have appeared at all. She revealed years later than Connery was so nervous on set that he kept messing up his delivery. 'He came out with other permutations like "Sean Bond, James Connery …"' Director Terence Young had to keep calling 'cut'. Eventually he decided that the only way to calm the actor down was with alcohol (Ian Fleming would have approved). Young suggested to Gayson that she take Connery for a drink, and when he was ready bring him back to deliver the line again. Post-booze, the take was perfect.

HONOR BLACKMAN

Her appearance as Pussy Galore in *Goldfinger* gave her the distinction of being the oldest Bond girl (39), a record that lasted all the way until 2015's *Spectre*, when 50-year-old Monica Bellucci played Lucia Sciarra. Indeed Blackman was also significantly older than *her* Bond (Sean Connery was 34 at the time of the film's release). The only other occasion this has happened apart from *Spectre* (Daniel Craig was 47) was in *On Her Majesty's Secret Service* (Diana Rigg 31, George Lazenby 30). Pussy Galore ticks any number of male fantasies.

According to the book she is a lesbian – until Bond gets hold of her, saying 'They told me you only liked women.' Her reply? 'I never met a man before.'

But don't go calling Blackman a Bond girl to her face. 'I hate that term,' she has said. 'They can call other people Bond girls, but I don't like it, for the simple reason that that character would have been a good character in any film, not just a Bond film. I consider Bond girls to be those ladies who took one look at Bond and fell on their backs – whereas Pussy Galore was quite a character.'

SHIRLEY EATON

As Jill Masterson, the other Bond girl in *Goldfinger*, she meets her death by being painted gold. An urban myth arose that Eaton had actually died during filming of the scene. What is true is that in *Diamonds Are Forever*, Lana Wood nearly died when filming the scene where her character, Plenty O'Toole, drowns by being tied to a concrete block in a swimming pool (the block slipped down the pool's sloping floor). In a cruel twist of fate, her sister, the actress Natalie Wood, really did die by drowning.

CLAUDINE AUGER

Auger played Domino in *Thunderball*. She and Bond meet underwater, wearing scuba gear, and hide behind some rocks. The next shot was going to be from above the water, where we see Domino's bikini floating on the surface, but this was thought to be too suggestive, so it was cut. Not even Bond works that fast.

DIANA RIGG

This actress, who played Teresa 'Tracy' di Vicenzo in *On Her Majesty's Secret Service,* enjoyed the unique privilege of becoming Bond's only wife (for a couple of hours). Spoiler alert: she cops it in the final scene.

As previously alluded to, there were rumours that Rigg didn't have the most cordial of relationships with new Bond George Lazenby, but she has always denied this. The deliberate garlic munching is explained by a comment a visiting reporter overheard when she shouted across the set before a love scene: 'I'm having garlic for lunch, George. I hope you are!'

MIE HAMA

Played Kissy Suzuki in *You Only Live Twice,* though you wouldn't know it, as for some reason the character's name is never actually mentioned. Interesting bluffing fact: she was the only Bond girl to bear our hero's child (in the novel).

JILL ST JOHN

Achieved fame as Tiffany Case, the first American Bond girl, in *Diamonds Are Forever.* Around that time, she had a relationship with Frank Sinatra. Bizarrely, her future husband, Robert Wagner, was in a relationship with Sinatra's daughter Tina. She has since said: 'Diamonds are forever. My youth is not.'

The character's name is explained in the novel. Her

father, so angry that she wasn't a boy, gave her mother a thousand dollars and a compact from Tiffany's before walking out.

Other Bond girls have names that reflect their lives. For example, Solitaire, from *Live and Let Die* (real name Simone Latrelle), excludes men from her life, while it has been suggested that *Casino Royale*'s Vesper Lynd is a pun on 'West Berlin' (say 'Lynd' with a silent 'd'). The character's loyalties are divided between the Soviet Union and the West.

You're never going to be a Bond girl if they can't fit your name on the poster.

JANE SEYMOUR

Chosen to bring Solitaire to life in *Live and Let Die*. It isn't a coincidence that Seymour shares a name with one of Henry VIII's wives; that was precisely the reason the actress chose her stage name. Her real moniker is Joyce Penelope Wilhelmina Frankenberg. You're never going to be a Bond girl if they can't fit your name on the poster. You can mention Seymour whenever people trot out the old myth about David Bowie's eyes being different colours. Bowie's weren't (it was merely that one pupil was permanently enlarged after a childhood fight, making that eye look darker) – but Seymour's are. Her right eye is brown, her left eye green.

BRITT EKLAND

Ekland played Bond's assistant, Mary Goodnight, in *The Man with the Golden Gun*. In real life, she hit all the right buttons with her quote: 'I said I don't sleep with married men, but what I meant to say was I don't sleep with *happily* married men.' She had hit more buttons the year before her Bond appearance, with her role in cult British horror film *The Wicker Man*. However, some of the legendary shots in which she dances naked around a bedroom were actually filmed using a body double. Ekland was prepared to show her breasts but not her bottom ('for me anything below the waist is private' – not a very Bond-ish sentiment). The Glasgow stripper hired to supply the derrière shots did not meet with Ekland's approval. 'The first I knew about it was when the film came out and then I was in a state of shock. Her bottom was much bigger than mine.'

HALLE BERRY

Her appearance as Jinx in *Die Another Day* made Berry the only Bond girl with an Oscar for Best Actress (achieved in *Monster's Ball*). Kim Basinger, however, who was Domino Petachi in the non-EON *Never Say Never Again*, got an Oscar for Best Supporting Actress (in *LA Confidential*).

EVA GREEN

Played Vesper Lynd in *Casino Royale*. In the shower scene, she was originally meant to be wearing only her underwear, but Daniel Craig pointed out that she would not have paused to take her clothes off, so she kept them on. Yes, gentlemen, you have Craig himself to blame for that one.

DAME JUDI DENCH

Arguably the most important 'Bond girl' of the lot, not least because she was his steely-eyed, no-nonsense boss for seven films (eight if you include her short *Spectre* cameo, a video message to 007). If Bond had ever struggled with the idea of serving a female M, all he would have had to do is remind himself that in real life, Dench is a Dame Commander of the Order of the British Empire. That would be enough to whip even the bolshiest of licensed assassins into shape. As Daniel Craig himself said: 'Judi Dench can say a hundred words and make them sound wonderful, but can also give one look and break your heart.'

ESSENTIAL
BOND MISCELLANY

A vital weapon in any bluffer's armoury is the casual (or seemingly casual) knack of dropping fascinating and little-known facts into any conversation involving your chosen area of bluffing expertise. Admittedly, most of this book provides exactly such information, but the following intriguing facts take you one step further, beyond the information you're expected to know, and reaching into the realms of material to which only an absolute expert might be privy.

But beware: you've got to drop your Bond nuggets subtly. Introduce 007 into the proceedings by a clever massaging of logic and causality and you'll impress people. Shoehorn him into every last sentence and they'll want to hit you – probably somewhere delicate with a carpet beater.

BOND AND THE SECOND WORLD WAR

The obvious link between Bond and the war is his actual wartime service. Bond entered the Royal Naval Volunteer Reserve (RNVR) in 1941 by claiming to be 19 (he was in fact two years younger). According to his *Times* obituary – given at the end of penultimate novel *You Only Live Twice*, and written by M because Bond is missing, presumed dead – he was accorded the rank of lieutenant in the Special Branch of the RNVR. It was 'a measure of the satisfaction his services gave to his superiors that he ended the war with the rank of Commander' (at the tender age of just 21).

But why mention something that any Bond fans worth their salt will probably already know? Point out instead that Bond uses the same gun (a Walther PPK 7.65mm), which fired the single most famous shot of the Second World War: the one with which Adolf Hitler killed himself.

BOND AND JEFFREY ARCHER

Although it's unlikely for someone as rigidly duty-bound as 007 to value any sort of association with a jailbird, there is nonetheless something that any Bond bluffer should know about his connection to a novelist who has sold more books than Fleming. Archer's penthouse flat overlooking the River Thames in London was previously owned by John Barry, composer of many of the Bond themes. When Barry first installed a telephone there, he arranged to choose his own number. The last three digits were (what else?) '007'. Archer elected to keep the number. Who can blame him?

BOND AND CRICKET

Bond is definitely not a team player, preferring individual sports – a practice that reflects his status as a loner. His *Times* obituary mentions that, while at school, he twice boxed as a lightweight, and founded the school's judo class. He also learned to ski at Kitzbühel in the Austrian Tyrol (inevitably he was brilliant) and played very good golf, with a handicap of nine.

Cricket might be one of the few team games sufficiently slow-paced to allow for Bond's prodigious daily cigarette consumption.

Cricket might be one of the few team games sufficiently slow-paced to allow for Bond's prodigious daily cigarette consumption. He does cut down to 20 on a particularly arduous mission, though.

The cricket connection comes via Bond's most persistent enemy, Blofeld. Fleming took the name from Thomas Blofeld, his Eton contemporary and fellow member of gentlemen's club Boodle's. Blofeld's son, Henry, went on to become a legendary cricket commentator, notably with the BBC's *Test Match Special* team. Your audience might enjoy the connection between an arch-villain bent on world domination and a charming old boy chiefly famed for saying 'my dear old thing' and eating cream cakes.

BOND AND THE ROYAL FAMILY

Bond's official link to HM Queen Elizabeth II is, of course, that he works for her government. Yet this doesn't prevent him in Fleming's very last Bond novel, *The Man with the Golden Gun,* from turning down her offer of a knighthood for his services. Mary Goodnight tries to change his mind, conjuring up the image of him visiting Buckingham Palace for the investiture. But Bond says he prefers to remain a 'Scottish peasant'.

A much more interesting association, however, is the role played by the Royal Family in ensuring that the best-known Bond girl of all, Pussy Galore, retained her name. American censors became nervous about the moniker, and asked that it be changed to 'Kitty Galore'. Bond publicist Tom Carlile was having none of this, so arranged to have Honor Blackman photographed with Prince Philip at the film's London premiere. Pictures duly appeared in the papers with the caption 'Pussy and the Prince', thereby scuppering the censors' plans.

More recently Bond has become a little closer to the Queen. In the most unexpected moment of the 2012 Olympics opening ceremony, the pair appeared to arrive by helicopter and then parachute into the Olympic Stadium, Her Majesty's pink bloomers alarmingly on display to billions of viewers worldwide.

BOND AND JFK

It seems only fitting that Bond and John F. Kennedy should have something in common. Unsurprisingly they did – not least the looks, the fame, the naval-hero background, the womanising. ...

In 1961, during the first weeks of his presidency, Kennedy revealed his favourite ten books of all time. Number nine was *From Russia with Love*. American sales of the Bond novels rocketed. Ian Fleming was keen to ensure that signed copies of his books went to both JFK and his brother Bobby. He also repaid the plug he had been given: 1962's *The Spy Who Loved Me* has a character opining: 'We need more Jack Kennedys', while in *The Man with the Golden Gun*, Bond reads JFK's own *Profiles in Courage*.

The most chilling connection, however, is the report that, on the night before his assassination, Kennedy was reading a Bond novel – as was Lee Harvey Oswald.

Fleming and Kennedy actually met in 1960, before JFK became president, at a dinner in Washington DC. Fleming made light-hearted suggestions about how Fidel Castro could be undermined, including dropping leaflets telling Cubans that beards were dangerous because they trapped radioactive dust and so caused impotence. There are convincing reports that the CIA subsequently tried to assassinate Castro with an exploding cigar, so perhaps Fleming's ideas weren't so fanciful after all.

The Cuban missile crisis was widely held to have assisted the success of *Dr No*, which was released at the same time.

BOND AND STING

The link between Bond and the former Newcastle teacher-turned-rock singer is that 'Every Breath You Take', probably Sting's most famous song, was written at the same desk as many of the James Bond novels.

The Police frontman was staying at Ian Fleming's Jamaican villa, *Goldeneye* (and sitting in Fleming's room, at Fleming's desk), at the time. You can add that the lyrics are entirely appropriate for a character with Bond's complicated view of women, and that he arguably gets a mention in the song: 'Every bond you break/Every step you take/I'll be watching you'.

BOND AND THE MAN WHO INSPIRED HIM

Special Operations Executive agent Lieutenant Colonel Geoffrey Gordon-Creed, DSO, MC (*see* page 22), was thought by some to be the most likely inspiration for Bond – principally because of his reputation for fearlessness and voracious sexual appetite. Until shortly before the outbreak of war, he was known as Geoffrey Eckstein, after his German stepfather.

A double agent? Unlikely. After an English public school education, Gordon-Creed took particular relish in killing German soldiers. Unless, of course, this was a particularly cunning double bluff. And don't forget that Bond's mother was Swiss, as were a number of Nazi war criminals. ...

BOND ANAGRAMS

Discussion of Bond can get rather earnest at times. Seriousness isn't a bad thing – after all, we know by now that one of your main arguments concerns the novels' superiority over the films precisely because they tackle important philosophical questions about the nature of good and evil. But too much seriousness *is* a bad thing. Should you ever need to lighten the tone of a conversation about 007, throw in some of these anagrams of Bond movie titles:

Dr No – *Ron D.* (And note that an anagram of 'Diamonds Are Forever' is *'Ron D. Overfeeds Maria'*.)

From Russia with Love – *Whole Fist, Mr Saviour*?

Goldfinger – *Dinglefrog*

You Only Live Twice – *Vote Nice, You Willy*!

The Man with the Golden Gun – *A Nightgowned Helmet Hunt*

Octopussy – *Sooty Cups*

The Living Daylights – *Lively Dating Thighs*

Tomorrow Never Dies – *Overtired Newsroom*

Die Another Day – *Hidden Toy Area.*

Begin each day by chasing a suspicious-looking passer-by. Be sure to make use of any unattended buses, tanks or moon buggies in the vicinity. Drive through as many brick walls as you can manage, and don't worry about the trail of havoc you leave behind you.

BEING BOND

For some people, knowing about Bond just isn't enough. Here's a guide on how to bluff others into believing that you actually are the most famous spy of all time.

AT WORK

* First things first: inform your boss that you will now only perform tasks deemed necessary to protect national security. It's your duty, after all.
* Insist on being referred to as a three-digit number. Colleagues may find it tiresome, but they're just jealous of your mystique.
* Turn the stationery cupboard into a secret weapons laboratory. If you can recruit an eccentric elderly scientist to live and work in there, all the better. Don't forget to visit him on a regular basis and test his patience by fiddling with his gadgets.
* Disappear for protracted lengths of time on 'special missions' to the most exotic locations possible. War zones, submarines, terrorist camps and tropical

islands are preferred, but if worse comes to worst, just hang out in Pret A Manger for an extra five minutes on your lunch break. You're a renegade, after all. And a lethal weapon.

* Never, ever lend anyone a pen. And never, ever borrow one, either. It will almost certainly explode.

* Flirt ruthlessly with a woman in the office. Any woman. Ideally, she should be your boss's quirkily named personal assistant, but any female colleague/ receptionist/cleaner will do. Stand slightly too close, lean against or over her workspace, and make leading remarks about her physical attributes. Be sure to swagger off before she can respond, and remember, feminism hasn't happened. * Get a hat. Spend endless hours practising skimming it across rooms, ensuring that it lands on a hatstand or your boss's head. What secretary wouldn't be impressed by such mastery? She'll love you even more for it.

* Prepare for all eventualities by keeping Speedos, a parachute and full ski apparel close at hand. Ideally, incorporate all three when choosing an outfit. You could be called upon to jump out of a plane at any moment (whether or not it's required). And don't forget to push the Queen out first.

* Rigorously train for that most vital of secret agent skills: emerging from the sea in slow motion, and ensuring that your trunks don't reveal too much private detail.

* Redesign your wardrobe to include sharp suits and silk pyjamas. *Only* sharp suits and silk pyjamas. You're deadly, but you're also stylish.

* Begin each day by chasing a suspicious-looking passer-by. Be sure to make use of any unattended buses, tanks or moon buggies in the vicinity. Drive through as many brick walls as you can manage, and don't worry about the trail of havoc you leave behind you. HM Treasury will pick up the tab. Under no circumstances break into a sweat, even if you get arrested for criminal damage.
* Finally, if someone mentions 'laser beams', leave immediately. You might find yourself tied to a table with one heading towards your licence to thrill. ...

AT PLAY

* Pepper every other sentence with a smutty innuendo. Phrases like 'rising to the occasion' and 'feeling a little cocky' are ideal, whether or not they fit the conversation. Charm like yours should never be restrained.
* Shun the standard drinking habits of your peers and request that all beverages be shaken, not stirred. Even when ordering a pint of shandy. Particularly when ordering a pint of shandy.
* When going to a party or a function, always wear a tuxedo and bow tie. Ensure that a shoulder holster is visible just above your cummerbund.
* When attending a wedding, hire an Aston Martin Vanquish for the day. Sod the expense – you could be shark bait tomorrow.
* If tapped on the shoulder, swivel around, drop to one knee and reach for your armpit. Do a couple of side-

rolls, get smartly to your feet, brush yourself down, and offer no explanation for your curious behaviour.

* Ring yourself regularly on your mobile. When you're certain that someone is close enough to overhear you, hiss into the mouthpiece that you're 'off duty', demand to know that the 'line is secure', pause for a moment, and then continue with as much meaningless jargon as you can remember, e.g., 'contra encryption', 'grey cell', 'clean skin', 'dead drop', 'friendly ghost', 'hard target', 'false flag', etc. In fact, just choose any combination of adjective and noun that springs to mind. Looking around your surroundings generally helps, e.g., 'locked window', 'closed door', 'open blind', 'drawn curtains', 'filthy food' and finish with a final flourish of 'It's my way, or no way. Do I make myself clear, M?'

* If someone offers you a tray of tired-looking canapés, express unqualified disgust and demand that they come back immediately with caviar, specifying that it must only be Beluga.

* Head for the most glamorous female in the room. Hold her firmly by the arm and propel her equally firmly toward the nearest French window saying: 'I think we have some unfinished business, Desiré Moorcock. Don't you agree?' Then kiss her cruelly on the lips.

* As you're lying gasping for breath on the floor, having just been kneed in the groin area, don't allow yourself to whimper. Simply say through gritted teeth: 'Shorry. Mishtaken identity.'

* When policemen or security guards come to remove you from the premises, run at speed towards the nearest exit. Assiduously practise Daniel Craig's running style

in advance: fingers pointing upwards, palms facing each other, arms pumping, mouth twisted in a smirk. If you can jump through an open window bringing the curtains down mid-defenestration, then award yourself extra bluffing points. Always ensure that you're on the ground floor before attempting this particular manoeuvre.

AT HOME

You don't have a home. Your backstory must remain a dangerous yet alluring mystery, even if you live with your mum in a bungalow by a roundabout. Should this come out, simply tell your friends that it's 'cover'. On the other hand, if you live by the above code, you're unlikely to have any friends.

ONE-LINERS

There is one further prerequisite to succeeding at becoming Bond, and that is the ability to deliver wry one-liners. The following examples should provide the necessary inspiration.

....

Verity I see you handle your weapon well.
Bond I have been known to keep my tip up.
Die Another Day

....

Tiger Tanaka Rule number two: in Japan, men come first, women come second.
Bond I just might retire here.
You Only Live Twice

Hugo Drax Why did you break up the encounter with my pet python?
Bond I discovered it had a crush on me.
Moonraker

....

Bond (*after knocking a heat lamp into a bath to electrocute a baddie*) Shocking! Positively shocking!
Goldfinger

....

Tatiana Romanova The mechanism is ... Oh James, James ... Will you make love to me all the time in England?
Bond Day and night. Go on about the mechanism.
From Russia with Love

....

Honey Ryder (*as she comes out of the sea*) Are you looking for shells too?
Bond No, I'm just looking.
Dr No

....

Minister of Defence Bond! What do you think you're doing?
Bond (*engaged in lovemaking*) Keeping the British end up, sir.
The Spy Who Loved Me

....

Bond I was wrong about you.
Christmas Jones Yeah, how so?
Bond I thought Christmas only comes once a year.
The World Is Not Enough

Bond (*in bed with his language tutor, and on the phone to Moneypenny*) I always enjoyed learning a new tongue.
Moneypenny You always were a cunning linguist, James.
Tomorrow Never Dies

....

Irma Bunt Is anything the matter, Sir Hilary?
Bond (*as girl is writing her room number on the inside of his thigh under the table*) Just a slight stiffness coming on. …
On Her Majesty's Secret Service

....

M Remember, 007, you're on your own.
Bond Well, thank you, sir. That's a great comfort.
Octopussy

....

Xenia Onatopp Enjoy it while it lasts.
Bond The very words I live by.
GoldenEye

....

Bond (*surprised by henchmen while in a state of undress with Plenty O'Toole*) Well, I'm afraid you've caught me with more than my hands up.
Diamonds Are Forever

....

Bond It appears we share the same passions: three, anyway.
Xenia Onatopp I count two: motoring and, uh, baccarat. I hope the third is where your real talent lies.
Bond One rises to meet a challenge.
GoldenEye

Tiffany Case (*pointing to her blonde wig*) Which do you prefer?
Bond Well, as long as the collar and cuffs match.
Diamonds Are Forever
....

Helga Brandt I've got you now.
Bond Well, enjoy yourself.
You Only Live Twice
....

Felix Leiter I give up. I know the diamonds are in the body, but where?
Bond Alimentary, Dr. Leiter...
Diamonds are Forever
....

Pussy Galore What happened? Where's Goldfinger?
Bond Playing his golden harp.
Goldfinger

There's no point in pretending that you know everything about Bond – nobody does – but if you've got this far and you've absorbed at least a modicum of the information and advice contained within these pages, then you will almost certainly know more than 99% of the rest of the human race about who Bond is and what he does. What you do with this information is up to you, but here's a suggestion: be confident about your new-found knowledge, see how far it takes you, but above all, have fun using it. After all, you are now a bona fide expert in the art of bluffing about the world's most infamous, ruthless, and enigmatic secret agent.

GLOSSARY

Bentley Make of car driven by Bond in the novels, as opposed to the Aston Martins/BMWs/Lotuses, etc., of the films. Customised and supercharged Bentleys, of course. The literary Bond wouldn't be seen dead in anything else.

Cameo One of the air stewardesses in *Die Another Day* is played by Roger Moore's daughter.

Cigars Roger Moore's contract as 007 specified that he be allowed an unlimited supply of hand-rolled Montecristo cigars while filming.

Coward, Noël Ian Fleming's friend (and neighbour in Jamaica). Was offered the role of villain in the first Bond film; his telegram reply said: '*Dr No*? No! No! No!'

Digital watch Bond first departs from the analogue version in *Live and Let Die*. They were all the rage once.

Disclaimer You know that bit in the end credits of a film that says 'No animals were harmed or mistreated in the making of this movie'? The first film it ever appeared in – not just the first Bond film, the first film full stop –

was *Never Say Never Again*. A horse had jumped off a cliff. Entirely safely, of course.

Exploding alarm clock Provided in *Licence to Kill*. Q tells Bond it's guaranteed not to wake up the person using it.

Fettes College The Edinburgh public school, often referred to as the 'Scottish Eton', attended by James Bond after he'd been expelled from Eton itself, following an incident with one of the maids. Fettes was also attended by Ian Fleming's father and, indeed, Tony Blair. A young Sean Connery was once the school's milkman.

Flick, Vic Guitarist responsible for the famous *dun-duddle-un-dun, dun-dun-dun* movie theme. Suggest he was chosen because his name made him sound like a Bond villain.

Fröbe, Gert German actor who starred as the villain in *Goldfinger* and Baron Bomburst in *Chitty Chitty Bang Bang*, the distinctly Bond-like story Fleming wrote for children. Which was the more over-the-top performance is debatable.

Gambon, Michael British actor approached to replace George Lazenby. He countered that he was bald; Cubby Broccoli retorted that so was Sean Connery. Gambon further countered that he had breasts like a woman; Broccoli replied that they'd use ice packs before the love scenes: 'Like we did with Sean.'

Geiger counter Bond uses one in *Dr No* as he searches a boat for radioactive rocks. His first gadget, and the last one to be remotely credible.

Key ring Used in *The Living Daylights*. It emits a cloud of stun gas when Bond whistles the opening bars of 'Rule

Britannia'. In real life that would be all very well until
he attended the Last Night of the Proms.

Laser The most famous Bond weapon of all was
one that was used against Bond rather than by him.
Goldfinger's laser accompanies his legendary 'No, Mr
Bond. I expect you to die' line. Although the beam was
a special effect added later, the table on which Bond is
strapped really was cut open by a blowtorch operated
from beneath. It gets rather close to Sean Connery's
'gentleman's region'. No wonder his acting in this scene
is particularly convincing.

Licence to Kill The title, in Italy, of *Dr No*. This created
a problem, of course, when *Licence to Kill* came out. So
they called that one *Private Revenge*.

M Head of Bond's Secret Service. Frederick Forsyth
put forward the theory that Fleming took the 'M'
from the first name of the first real head of MI6,
Captain Sir Mansfield Cumming. Get bonus bluffing
points for referring to not one thriller writer but two.
Then go one better and suggest that the prototype for
M was Maxwell Knight, the spymaster who recruited
Fleming as his agent.

Pinewood Studios Long-time home to the Bond
movies. Its '007 Stage' is, at 59,000 square feet, the largest
in Europe. This dates from *The Spy Who Loved Me*, whose
set designer Ken Adam warned Cubby Broccoli that there
wasn't a stage big enough for the film's set pieces. The
producer's response was simple: 'Then build it.'

Portable photocopier Used by George Lazenby in *On
Her Majesty's Secret Service*. Well, it was state-of-the-art
at the time. Bond copies some documents, then, just

for good measure, the centrefold from a nearby issue of *Playboy.*

Q He who traditionally arms Bond with his high-tech gadgets at the beginning of an assignment. Stands for 'Quartermaster'. Q was not a character in the novels, although in the first one, *Casino Royale*, it is 'Q Branch' that supplies 007's gadgets.

Sakata, Harold Actor who played Oddjob in *Goldfinger*. Represented the USA in the 1948 Olympics as a weightlifter. Well, it wasn't going to be the 100-metre hurdles, was it?

Seagal, Steven Before he grunted and glared his way across our screens as a B-list star himself, Seagal was the martial-arts coach on *Never Say Never Again.*

Seagull snorkel suit Not to be confused with Seagal, above. Put a seagull on top of a snorkel and you'll be able to trick your way into a drugs-manufacturing complex. At least you will if you're Sean Connery in *Goldfinger*.

SMERSH The Soviet counter-intelligence body fought by Bond. The acronym is short for *SMERt SHpionam* – literally, 'death to spies' in Russian. (Either that, or someone's carelessly leaned on your keyboard.) The real-life (and much smaller) SMERSH was founded in the 1940s by the Red Army. Joseph Stalin was responsible for the name.

SPECTRE Global criminal conspiracy headed by Ernst Stavro Blofeld. Stands for Special Executive for Counter-intelligence, Terrorism, Revenge and Extortion. Unlike SMERSH, it's fictional.

Stephens, Toby Much underrated as sinister North Korean megalomaniac Gustave Graves in *Die Another Day*. He is of particular interest to bluffers for being the only Bond villain to have a mother who is a real life Dame (Maggie Smith) and a father who was a theatrical knight (Sir Robert Stephens).

Tuxedo Pierce Brosnan's 007 contract forbade him from wearing a tux in any other film. That's why in *The Thomas Crown Affair,* when he dances with Rene Russo at a formal ball, his bow tie is untied, thereby getting round the clause.

Universal Exports Fictional company name used by Bond's Secret Service as a cover for its activities. Very fitting, as by the 1970s Britain's industrial decline was so marked that just about its only remaining profitable exports were the Bond films.